# KNIFEMAKING

A Bladesmithing Guide on Forging Knives and Crafting Knife Sheaths with Simple Tools for Beginners

By Michael Peterson

# KNIFEMAKING

## © Copyright 2021 - All rights reserved.

The content contained within this book may not be reproduced, duplicated or transmitted without direct written permission from the author or the publisher.

Under no circumstances will any blame or legal responsibility be held against the publisher, or author, for any damages, reparation, or monetary loss due to the information contained within this book. Either directly or indirectly.

Legal Notice:

This book is copyright protected. This book is only for personal use. You cannot amend, distribute, sell, use, quote or paraphrase any part, or the content within this book, without the consent of the author or publisher.

Disclaimer Notice:

Please note the information contained within this document is for educational and entertainment purposes only. All effort has been executed to present accurate, up to date, and reliable, complete information. No warranties of any kind are declared or implied. Readers acknowledge that the author is not engaging in the rendering of legal, financial, medical or professional advice. The content within this book has been derived from various sources. Please consult a licensed professional before attempting any techniques outlined in this book.

By reading this document, the reader agrees that under no

circumstances is the author responsible for any losses, direct or indirect, which are incurred as a result of the use of information contained within this document, including, but not limited to, — errors, omissions, or inaccuracies.

# KNIFEMAKING

## Table of Contents

**Introduction** .................................................................. ix

**Chapter One: A Brief History of Knifemaking** ............. 1

    Early Cutting Tools ........................................................ 2

    Knifemaking in Europe ................................................. 4

    Knifemaking in the Americas ........................................ 4

**Chapter Two: Basic Knifemaking Tools** ..................... 10

    Basic Equipment .......................................................... 11

    Bonus Tool: Social Media ........................................... 23

**Chapter Three: Setting Up Your Knifemaking Workshop** .................................................................. 26

    Location, Location, Location ...................................... 27

    Size ............................................................................... 28

    Storage and Organization of Your Shop ..................... 29

    Light and Power .......................................................... 32

    Small Equipment Storage ............................................ 33

    Large Equipment Storage and Considerations ........... 33

**Chapter Four: How to Design Your Knife** ................. 39

Parts of a Knife ..................................................40

Common Knife Shapes ......................................44

Fixed Blade versus Folding Blade .......................54

Computer Programs for Knife Designing ..................56

Adobe Illustrator CC ..........................................57

Adobe Photoshop ...............................................57

Autodesk Inventor ..............................................58

Autodesk Fusion 360 ..........................................58

CorelDraw Graphics Suite ..................................58

**Chapter Five: Choosing Your Steel ............................ 61**

What is a Good Steel for Making Knives? ................62

All About Steel—The Basics ...............................63

Properties of Steel ..............................................64

Steel Nomenclature ............................................66

Alloy Additions ..................................................72

Other Steels for Knifemaking ..............................79

Where to Acquire Steel .......................................82

Reclaimed Metal ................................................83

Scrap Metal Sources...........................................................87

Annealing Steel................................................................88

**Chapter Six: Forging and Heating Metal**...................91

Sources of Heat................................................................93

Kiln....................................................................................93

Forges...............................................................................94

Furnaces............................................................................94

Ovens................................................................................94

DIY Heat-Treating Oven................................................95

DIY Propane Forge.........................................................99

Choosing the Fuel for Your Forge..............................103

The Forging Process......................................................105

Managing the Heat........................................................105

Quenching......................................................................108

Water Quenching..........................................................109

Brine Quenching............................................................109

Caustic Soda...................................................................110

Mineral Oil.....................................................................110

Vegetable Oils ................................................................110

**Chapter Seven: Step-by-Step Bladesmithing ............113**

Producing the Knife from the Blank........................114

Drilling the Knife Blank ..........................................115

Getting the Final Knife Shape ..................................116

Grinding the Bevel ..................................................118

Sanding the Blade ....................................................125

Heat-Treating to the Critical Point...........................127

Quenching in Oil.....................................................128

Tempering Your Knife .............................................130

Final Sanding for Finish...........................................131

**Chapter Eight: Creating a Knife Handle and Sheath ................................................................................. 134**

Sizing the Handle ....................................................135

Cutting the Scales and Drilling the Pin Holes ..........135

Cutting and Inserting Pins .......................................136

Sand the Handle to Shape........................................137

Glue the Scales to the Tang .....................................138

Peen the Pins...........................................................139

Shape the Handle to the Tang .................................. 140

Finishing the Handle ................................................ 140

Crafting a Sheath .................................................... 142

Tools You'll Need ................................................... 143

**Chapter Nine: Maintaining Your Knife ....................151**

What to Do for Knife Care.................................... 152

**Chapter Ten: Knifemaking as a Business ................ 159**

Treat Knifemaking Like a Business........................... 160

Invest in Equipment................................................ 160

Identify Your Niche ................................................ 161

Communicate ........................................................ 161

Create Your Competitive Advantage ........................ 162

Delegate ................................................................ 162

Professional Photography........................................ 163

Stay Grounded ....................................................... 163

**Final Words ................................................................. 165**

# INTRODUCTION

If you're looking for a hobby where you can express yourself creatively in almost infinite ways, then knifemaking is just what you're looking for. You will be amazed by the fact that you can make your own working knife.

# KNIFEMAKING

You might not have ever thought about where knives are made, or if you're like me, before I got into knifemaking, I just thought they were all made in a factory. I've learned a lot since then, and one of things I've discovered is that there is almost nothing more satisfying than making knives.

It takes patience, but if you've got that, you can develop all the skills you need to make knives yourself. Knifemaking lets you explore your creativity as you seek perfection in the finished product. No one really ever achieves perfection, not even the pros, but the closer you get to it, the more satisfied you'll feel about the work you've done. And, of course, if you're selling your work, you'll get more money for your finished product.

What's even better about knifemaking as a hobby is that it doesn't really take a lot of tools. You can actually make high quality knives with just a few good tools. The most important tools, however, are your imagination and patience, and with those, you'll soon be achieving your knifemaking goals.

Just imagine how impressed your friends and family will be when you show them the knives you've made, and more importantly, just imagine how good you'll feel about yourself. Bladesmithing is true artistry. It takes talent and skill to produce knives that will catch the eye of collectors, but you can do it, and I want to help.

I've designed this book to help the beginner get started in this amazing craft. I've spent many years making knives myself, so I know all the pitfalls, and I can help you avoid them. What's more, I've designed this book to be easy to read and chocked full of tips for the beginner.

We'll begin by discussing a little about the history of knifemaking, and then we'll move on to the kinds of tools you'll need. After that, I'll walk you through the basics of setting up your own workshop, choosing the best metal for your blades, and designing, forging, and grinding your knife to produce the best blade possible.

I'll also take you through the basics of creating the knife handle and sheath. Everything you need to know to get started in this fun and interesting hobby is presented in the pages to follow. Before you know it, you'll be designing and producing quality knives, and that's something that should make you proud.

This is a great hobby for anyone who's looking for a creative outlet that offers endless design possibilities. Not only are there various blade shapes and sizes to consider, you can let your creativity go wild when designing the sheath. As you get into this hobby, you'll see just how much artistry it involves, and the end product will be something practical you can use in everyday life.

Knifemaking is a great skill to have for anyone who likes to 'do it yourself.' With a few tools, a workshop, and your imagination, you can be designing and making knives that you can use, sell, or just display.

There's nothing more satisfying than making something yourself, and when you realize that you're using skills that our ancestors developed more than 8,000 years ago, you'll really feel like a skilled craftsman. So, what are we waiting for? Let's get started on making those blades!

# CHAPTER ONE

# A BRIEF HISTORY OF KNIFEMAKING

To truly appreciate the value of knifemaking, it's helpful to understand a little about the history of the craft. Humans have been producing sharp-edged tools for millions of years. In fact, it's one of the most important skills that helped our ancestors survive and thrive.

Today, of course, there are knives for every kind of purpose, from beautiful professional knives made with stainless steel and a high carbon content to common scissors for everyday use in the household. But, all of these have been thousands of years in the making.

# KNIFEMAKING

## Early Cutting Tools

As far as archaeologists can tell, our human ancestors first began using stone tools to cut animal tissue and bones around 2.5 million years ago. Since that time, cutting tools have been made from stone, ivory, horns, antlers, and then, around 6500 BC, humans began using metal tools.

At first, the metals used were too soft for either hunting or cooking. These early metals included copper, lead, and gold. Even blending them with other types of metal to make what are called alloys didn't completely solve the problem of softness.

In 4000 BC, however, the Egyptians discovered a material that is still today considered the sharpest cutting material in the world. It's called obsidian, and it's produced by a volcanic eruption. Obsidian is a kind of volcanic glass that has a sharp cutting edge, and in our modern world, it is the favored material for a scalpel blade. It creates a clean cut that results in faster healing.

The Egyptians also discovered how to make sharp knives from flint, and their discoveries were celebrated artistically with the production of beautiful ceremonial knives. The technology either spread or was independently discovered in many parts of the world around this time.

Around 1000 BC, the discovery of iron gave knifemaking its real boost. Iron gave knives what other metals could not, namely strength and durability. Knives made from iron were great for cutting and chopping, and because iron was readily available, it was inexpensive. The main drawback was that it is prone to rusting. It can also be too malleable.

Those problems were solved, however, around 700 BC, when metalsmiths discovered that adding carbon to iron—which makes steel—helped improve the final product. Added to that discovery were improvements in furnaces that helped produce durable, flexible metal that could take and hold its sharp edge.

## Knifemaking in Europe

The technology for making knives was soon present all over the world. Sheffield became the British center for knifemaking in the 14th century, but by the 16th century, the French were the leaders of the knifemaking world.

By that time, kitchen knives had been developed as a by-product from daggers and knife weaponry, and table knives, spoons, and forks had become commonplace in Europe. The problem was that carbon steel was too soft and too easily pitted and got discolored by foods high in acid. That meant that cutlery required careful production techniques and immediate drying when wet.

By the early 20th century, metalsmiths had more control of their furnaces and they were able to add chrome to stainless steel. That prevented rust and discoloration, and it also resulted in a tough blade with a sharp edge that held up even in wet conditions.

At this point in time, the Germans were considered the master cutlers in the West. Solingen had been the powerhouse for knifemaking ever since 1731, and the company's knives were considered second to none.

## Knifemaking in the Americas

The history of knifemaking in the Americas is perhaps represented by a few iconic knife styles. In the United States, the Bowie knife was made famous by James Bowie. James Bowie was a famous Western knife fighter who died in the historic battle of the Alamo. The Alamo was a fort in Texas that was captured by a Mexican army garrison in December of 1835 during the early stages of the Texas war for independence from Mexico.

The knife designed by Bowie was made for fighting, and it was such a good design that it is considered to be the basic foundation for the majority of modern fighting knives. It was a simple design that used a large, straight blade with a handle. No one would call this an elegant weapon, but it is a great, long-lasting, all-purpose utility blade known for its durability.

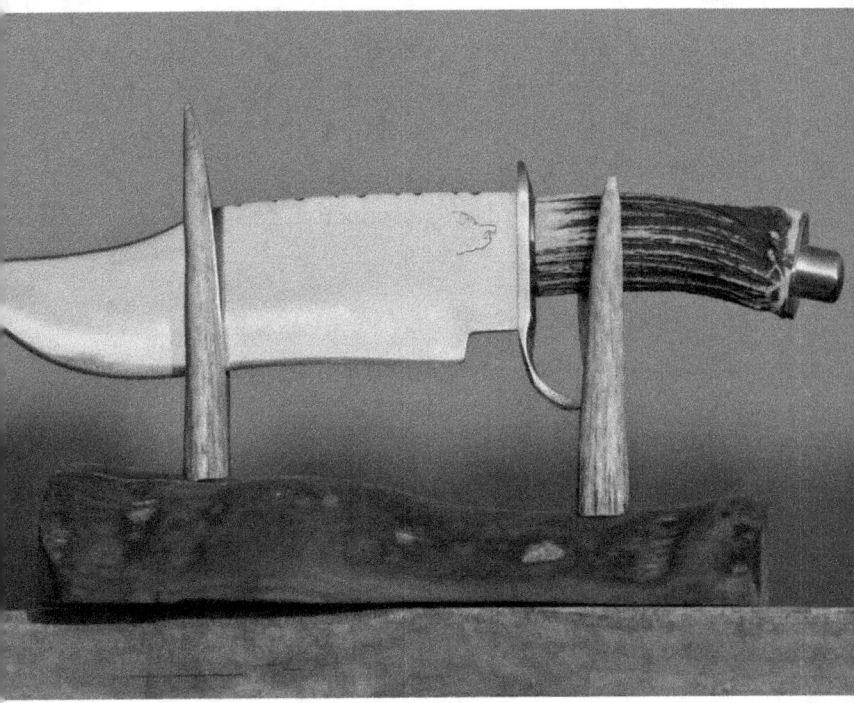

Another well-known American knife is the Buck knife. In 1902, Hoyt Buck—who was a blacksmith apprentice in Kansas—discovered a way to temper steel so that it would hold an edge longer. His initial experiments used hoes for raw material, but after he retired in the early 1940s, he started making knives for the servicemen in his local area for free.

The servicemen brought him the materials, and he produced small, fixed-blade knives. He ultimately produced a design called the 119 Special, and it is this knife that is known as the modern day Buck knife. His craftsmanship also resulted in the first upgrade of the M9 bayonet.

Hoyt and his wife moved to San Diego in 1945 to be closer to their son, and together, father and son started H.H. Buck and Son, Inc., on April 7, 1961. By 1964, they had designed the 110 Folding Hunter knife that became world-famous as a dependable, production-made folding, lock-back knife.

Part of its allure is that it is the right size for many different kinds of uses. Ranchers, soldiers, fishermen, policemen, hunters, and even electricians can all use this knife for their varied purposes. Buck knives are still made in Post Falls, Idaho today, and they are considered among the best in the world.

In South America, one iconic knife is the Faca or Facón which was used by gauchos. The Faca is a knife that falls somewhere in between the Bowie knife and some of the more decorative fighting knives of the past. The blade is large and sturdy, but it is also decorated with often elaborate designs.

The Faca is about the size of a chef's knife, and it was frequently used to settle disputes between men. These disputes were not fights to the death; rather, the men would slash each other on the face until one conceded defeat. That usually happened because they had so much blood in their eyes that they couldn't see.

## Asian Knifemaking

While there are many different Asian traditions, the Chinese and Japanese made specific, meaningful contributions to knifemaking. This was due in part to their cuisine. Eating small bites of food with chopsticks required that the meal be cut beforehand.

The result of their culinary preferences was a large, carbon-steel cleaver with a square end which became the knife of choice for cutting food. It was the standard knife in the Chinese kitchen for centuries, and it is still used today though now it is made of polished stainless steel.

Among the Japanese knives, two stand out: the kasumi and the honyaki. These knives were derived from the traditional manufacture of samurai swords. Kasumi knives are made through a complex process involving the heating of high carbon-steel and soft iron together. Once hot, they are hammered flat, folded, and then hammered flat and folded again. This is done by hand and is repeated at various angles with many layers.

A shimmering, subtle pattern results when the blade is polished. This is called *kasuminagashi*, which means the 'floating mist.' It is the same kind of effect seen on metals produced in Damascus, Syria around 400 BC with a laminating technique that produced what became known as the Damascene effect.

Honyaki knives are considered higher quality and are made completely from high carbon-steel. They are, however, more difficult to keep sharp and to use. Today, the knifemaking craft in Japan is still done by small family businesses. Their craftsmanship exceeds their volume, but they make some of the best knives in the world.

This brief history helps give you an idea of what has gone into the tradition of knifemaking. It is surely a long, honored history. You are following in the footsteps of literally millions of people across thousands of years of time. That's part of what makes knifemaking such a great hobby. The sense of being part of something that has been a human cultural tradition for millennia.

# KNIFEMAKING

## Chapter Summary

In this chapter, we've discussed a brief history of knifemaking. Specifically, we've covered the following topics:

- Early cutting tools;
- Western knifemaking traditions;
- The Bowie knife;
- The Buck knife;
- East Asian knifemaking traditions;
- Chinese cutlery;
- Japanese knives.
- 

In the next chapter you will learn about the tools you will need to get started in this fascinating hobby.

# CHAPTER TWO

# BASIC KNIFEMAKING TOOLS

As with any skill, you need the right tools for the job. It's critical for knifemaking to have what you need to produce a quality product. It can be expensive if you decide to go pro, but you can get started with a few essential, inexpensive tools.

It's a good rule of thumb that simple projects require simple tools. To get started, you want to just buy what you need for the job. Later, if you're interested in advancing to the next stage, you can buy some more elaborate types of tools. To get started, let's look at the top 11 tools that knifemakers need. The first eight are basic tools that you can use to get started, and then, we'll discuss three more advanced tools to help you get even better at the trade.

## Basic Equipment

The following tools are the basic equipment you will need to get started in knifemaking. Each tool is discussed along with its approximate price, but of course, prices may be different depending on where you find the tool.

## Tool #1: File

The first tool you need is often considered the metalsmith's best friend, a good file. Files don't cost a lot, and you can do a lot of great things with this basic tool. You can, for example, grind, finish, and smooth your knife.

For different jobs, you'll want files that are of various grit sizes and shapes, but many knifemakers started with just a file. What's more, they are inexpensive, usually less than $10, and they can be found at any metal store. You will have to work with them manually, but even though you might later replace them with power tools, you'll still want to keep a good set of files around.

### Tool #2: Clamps

If you had a second set of hands, you wouldn't need these, but unless that's the case, you'll want clamps to secure the knife as you work. You'll actually need more than one pair of clamps for different situations. Luckily, they are inexpensive, and so, you can get several at once. You'll want to begin with c-clamps and welders, and then, you can also utilize bar clamps, pipe clamps, one-handed clamps, and many other types as well. They typically start at just $10 depending on which type you're looking at.

### Tool #3: Hacksaw

You will need a hacksaw that has a high-quality blade since it is one of the most important tools in your kit. It will help you to cut and shape the steel. In fact, the entire knifemaking process starts with a hacksaw. While you can use power tools to do the job more quickly, they can't get into those tight corners you'll need them to get into. Luckily, you can find hacksaws online for just $20, but you'll want to order a few spare blades too. Often you can find kits that include several spares.

### Tool #4: Bench Vise

If you're going to be working with metal, you're going to need minimally one bench vise. It's an essential part of your basic toolkit. There are many options for bench vises to choose from. A good one to start with is a brand that has a 360-degree swivel base adjustment. This will allow you to reorient what you're working on by simply swiveling the base.

You can find a good bench vise for around $100. If that's a little steep for you, you can also usually buy a good used one. The best size to get is five inches, but you'll also eventually want even bigger ones than that. It is also helpful to get some soft jaw caps that will protect the knife as you work. These are typically made out of rubber, leather, plastic, copper, or aluminum, and they cost around $20 online.

### Tool #5: Drill

You can begin with a hand drill that has bits capable of drilling steel, but as you advance, you'll probably want to upgrade to a drill press. It's much easier to work with. You might even decide to start with a used drill press, but you'll want to make sure it has a drill vise. This tool will allow you to be more precise which will ultimately save you on time.

Hand drills cost approximately $30. A ten inch drill press can be found at some stores for around $121, and Cobalt drill bits will run you about $30 online. You can find a smaller—four inch—drill press vise for around $17. That will work just fine too.

### Tool #6: Sharpening Stone

The final step in the knifemaking process is to sharpen the knife. There are many different options available for sharpening stones, and the prices range from a mere $20 to $200 or more. There are several factors to take into consideration including the stone shape, grit textures, and size. The price varies according to the type of stone used; most knifemakers like diamond sharpening stones, but there are also ceramic stones, Arkansas stone, and water stones. It's really up to you which material you find to be the most suitable for your purposes.

**Tool #7: Dremel or Similar Rotary Tool**

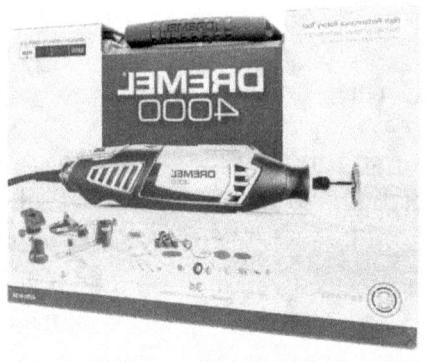

A rotary tool like Dremel is great for cutting materials, detail grinding, cleaning rust, jeweling, or otherwise customizing your knife. Dremel uses mounted, abrasive cones, points and bits, and small rubber or cut-off wheels to get the job done. The favored Dremel among knifemakers is the Dremel 400, which costs about $77. If you search online, you can sometimes find even better deals.

You might also want to buy a handpiece or flex shaft attachment. This is a great accessory that allows you to work without having to hold the motor unit in your hand. That will free you up to do more precise work.

**Tool #8: Safety Gear**

Whenever you're working on grinding, cutting, or heat-treating metal of any kind, you'll want to use safety gear. This includes safety glasses to protect your eyes, dust masks or respirators to avoid inhaling anything toxic, and gloves for protecting your hands.

Remember that you're cutting, grinding, or heating metal, and there are always small pieces of debris generated from this kind of work. You don't want one of those pieces flying into your eyes or hands, and you don't want to inhale hazardous dust particles.

Typically, personal protective gear is cheap and can be found at various hardware stores. The most expensive piece of protective gear is a respirator, but it works far better than just a dust mask. A high-quality respirator will run you around $100.

It's also essential for knifemakers to have a fire extinguisher available in the workshop. You're forging steel, and you don't want any part of your workspace to catch fire. You can purchase a five pound rechargeable fire extinguisher for under $50.

**A Few Other Basic Tools**

Aside from the specialty tools listed above, there are several other basic tools you'll need. Many of these you

# KNIFEMAKING

might already have, but if not, they're easy to find and inexpensive to purchase.

- **Hammer**: You'll need at least one hammer. The most handy size is a 20 ounce ball pein.

- **Anvil**: You'll need a good anvil for shaping your blades with the hammer.

- **Center Punch**: This will help make your job much easier. It will keep the bits on target and the result will be a more professional looking knife.

- **Wood Rasp**: This will help you to shape the handle of the knife.

- **Ruler**: It's best to have a stainless steel ruler that has both inches and centimeters. You'll use this a lot.

- **Permanent Markers**: Get several with a fine or ultra fine tip. These will be among your best tool friends.

- **Assorted Sandpaper**: This will help with the shaping, smoothing, and polishing you'll need to do. You want to get some wet/dry sandpapers that range from 60 to 600 grit.

- **Wood Blocks**: Hardwood blocks are good for holding sandpaper. You can just cut a few scraps of oak or maple into squares and dowels of different diameters. You'll find these very helpful.

**Advanced Equipment**

While the basic tools discussed above are all you need to get started in the hobby of knifemaking, as you do more and more, you'll probably want to invest in some more advanced pieces of equipment. This is particularly true if you want to make the move from being a hobbyist to being a professional knifemaker. The following tools will help you to achieve your goal to become a true master knifemaker.

**Tool #9: Belt Grinder**

If you're serious about going pro, you'll want to get a 2 inch by 72 inch industrial belt sander for knives. These are made specifically for professionals, and buying the smaller 1 inch by 42 inch grinder isn't an option for the professional. It's better to wait than to buy the less expensive, smaller grinder. The smaller version just simply isn't capable of doing the job you need it to do.

The price of a professional-grade belt grinder varies significantly based on several factors.

- Motor power: Don't drop below 1HP if you are planning on grinding tick and long steel bars;
- Motor speed: You want to get variable speed since it is the best option for this purpose;
- Wheel speed;
- Wheel size: Usually, you want a size of eight inches, but you can purchase any size you need;
- Body material;
- Accessories;
- Quick-release belt mechanism;
- Tracking adjustments.

While the final price depends on the choices you make for the above factors, you can find a belt grinder for approximately $600 plus shipping. The higher quality models can run you as much as $3,000, but you can sometimes find a good used one online. The best brands to consider are Kalamazoo, Grizzly, Bader, Coote, Wilmont, KMG, and NRT.

## Tool #10: The Flat Disc Machine

This machine helps you create a tight fit between two matching surfaces. This is something the belt grinder can't really do for you. To get that tight fit, you'll need the disc to run 'true' and you'll need the on/off switch to be foot-operated.

Without a foot-operated switch, you'll end up with one end of your material being slightly tapered because that's where it made first contact with the disc or the running belt. If you have a foot switch, you can press the material against the disc before you turn the machine on. This way, you can get an exact fit between surfaces.

The best discs to use for this machine are threaded aluminum discs, and you'll need an arbor on which you can mount them. You'll also want a paper-cutting jig that can cut full sheets of sandpaper. You'll be cutting them into strips and using them for hand finishing your knives.

## Tool #11: Heat-Treating Oven

Heat-treating refers to exposing the metal blade to a certain temperature for a minimal amount of time. This is done to make the blade stronger as well as giving it the ability to hold an edge and respond to the forces to which it is exposed. In short, heat-treating has been successful if the blade is able to do the work for which it was made.

If a knife blade is too soft, for example, it won't stay sharp, and it also might bend as it is being used. If it is too hard, on the other hand, it can chip or even break during normal use. Just like Goldilocks said, you want a treatment that is 'just right.'

To achieve the right heat-treatment, you need three elements: heating, cooling, and time. Even a slight variation in temperature can produce a big effect on the blade. It takes the right combination of temperature and time to produce the best results, and that often depends on a number of factors like the type of steel, for example.

Quenching is the heating/cooling method, and it involves heating the blade to a certain point and then cooling it quickly. That will produce steel that is hard, brittle, and full of stress and is known as martensite. Martensite is typically not suitable for a knife. By lowering the temperature, you will soften the metal and relieve the stress. The low temperature treatment—usually between 375 and 500 degrees Fahrenheit—is called tempering, and it results in a usable product.

As you can see, this is the most important and demanding process you'll do when making a knife. Many knifemakers outsource this, and if you would like to do that, the shops where you bought your steel might offer that service. If you're serious about being a knifemaker, however, you'll need to master heat-treating, and for that, you'll need an oven. This is also known as a heat-treating furnace or a kiln.

Any blade longer than two to four inches will require heat-treating with a constant temperature of 1000 degrees. Getting that steady temperature can be tricky since the middle of the blade might be at the right temperature but the other parts could still be too cool. You need all parts of the blade to reach these temperatures in order to get consistency in hardness. If you don't get that consistency, that can cause the blade to fail because it won't hold the edge.

To get that consistency, you need a heat-treating oven. Because the oven's function is to achieve a specific, high temperature and keep it constant, you'll want it to have manual or digital temperature control as well as a reliable controller.

The capacity and size of the oven depends on the kind of blade you're heating. Temperatures are typically set at 2350 degrees Fahrenheit and 2000 degrees Fahrenheit.

To get an oven that can achieve these high temperatures constantly, it will cost you, but the price also depends on the oven's size. Ovens that have a chamber measuring 6.5 inches by 4.25 inches with a height of 18 inches will run you approximately $1,200. It's also important to note that these ovens are electric, and they draw lots of electricity.

You'll also need industrial stainless steel foil and ceramic racks for your oven. You'll use the racks to position the blades in the oven, and you'll use the heat-treat foil to protect them from discoloration and scaling.

If the costs are just too much for you as a beginner, you can also make a fire brick forge. It's a simple way to get the job done. There are several websites that have pictures and instructions for making a forge yourself.

Basically, you'll need two fire bricks, in which you'll drill out the internal chamber. You'll then mount the bricks in a metal bracket frame and drill a hole in the side of the bricks. You'll pass your propane burner through the hole, and you've now got an oven for heat-treating your blades.

The following materials are good for a two brick forge:

- **Swirl Tip Torch**: This type of torch swirls the flames to avoid focusing the heat on just one spot;

- **LPG or MAPP Gas**: This comes in a bottle, and you'll want two so that you don't run out of gas in the middle of a heat treat. These are basically the same as those camping style propane bottles.

- **Vegetable Oil**: You'll need at least two gallons, and this will be put in a metal container to act as your quench tank.

- **Gloves**: These should be leather to protect your hands from the heat. You don't want nylon over knuckles, as some gloves have, since that can melt and leave you with a bad burn.

- **Magnet**: This can be helpful for manipulating the metal.

- **Tongs**: You won't want to touch the red-hot blade with your hands, even with gloves on. The tongs will allow you to grab the hot metal safely.

- **Thermometer**: You'll want to have a thermometer available to make sure you're reaching the optimal temperatures.

-

**Bonus Tool: Social Media**

One of the most important tools you'll need if you're planning on going pro is a way to promote your work as well as have a little fun. You'll want to create some kind of social media account where you can ask for opinions, get advice, get 'Likes' from other knifemakers, learn new things, and improve on your ideas.

It's also a great way to sell your knives. You can promote posts featuring pictures of your work to people interested in knives and knifemaking. You can also find things you might need—tools or heat-treating services for example. In short, social media is a great way to get the word out about your work, sell your services or knives, and just be a part of the knifemaking community in general. To go pro, you need to consider this as an essential tool.

With these tools in your workshop, you can get started on your first blades. Later chapters will discuss more specifics about designing and making knives, but this is the minimal equipment you'll need to get the job done. You don't necessarily have to have the advanced equipment, but as you get more involved in this fascinating hobby, you'll probably want to have more equipment so you don't have to outsource some vital steps in the process.

## Chapter Summary

In this chapter, we've discussed the basic equipment you'll need to get started in the knifemaking hobby. Specifically, we've discussed the following topics:

- The basic equipment you'll need to get started;
- Average prices for the basics;
- Advanced equipment for serious knifemakers;
- Average prices for the more advanced equipment.

In the next chapter you will learn how to set up your workshop so you can get started making knives.

# CHAPTER THREE

# SETTING UP YOUR KNIFEMAKING WORKSHOP

When you're setting up your workspace for knifemaking, there are several things you'll want to keep in mind. You'll want the process to be as easy as possible, and that means having all the tools you need where they make the most sense with respect to the order of procedures.

As you're moving from one step to the next, you'll want to have the tools you need nearby and easy to access. You also don't want to be in the middle of doing something and be unable to find the tool you need. That can actually end up ruining the blade you're working on. That's why it's important to give some thought to the setup of your workshop.

You'll want to have a place for everything and everything in its place to be precise. That way, you always know where your tools are, and you won't have to go digging through drawers to find what you need. You want everything to be readily available.

Finally, most knifemakers start out in a small space for their hobby. If that's your situation, you'll want to know how to maximize that space so you can fit everything you need in an orderly manner. Here's what you'll need to help make it as easy as possible to have more fun and less frustration.

**Location, Location, Location**

As the saying goes, it's all about location. When you're setting up a workshop of any kind, you'll want to consider where is the best place to put it. It's important to think about the fact that you want it to be somewhere that it's not going to matter if that area becomes dusty or noisy.

You'll also want to consider the climate in your workshop. If it's located outside of your main house (probably the case for knifemaking), you might need to take steps to keep it warm enough in winter and cool enough in summer. You want to stay comfortable and not feel as though you don't want to work on your projects because it's too cold or too hot in your workshop.

Additionally, you will be working with some hazardous materials when you're making knives. You'll likely (at least eventually) have a forge, and that means you may not want to have your knifemaking workshop inside your home. Even though it's located outside your main house, you'll still also want to make sure it's well-ventilated.

It's also important to take standard fire safety precautions for your workshop. A fire extinguisher is the minimal requirement. Because you're working with fire, you'll also want to make sure your workshop has two exits in case something happens. At least one exit should be to the outside so that you can easily bring in your materials as needed. The other fire exit can be a window, but it needs to be large enough to allow you to get out easily and quickly.

### Size

No one ever complains that their workshop is too big, and in fact, you'll want as much space as you can find. You're going to need to include a sizable workbench as well as a few larger pieces of equipment. You also just want to feel as though you have the space you need to work. You'll need to be able to move around the workspace easily and have enough space that the hot metal you may be carrying in the tongs won't hit anything flammable.

You'll also want to make sure you have a sizable door in your shop. That will be a big advantage for bringing in equipment and materials for the work you're doing. Usually, the bigger the door the better.

## Storage and Organization of Your Shop

You want to have everything stored in a place that makes sense to you, and where you can get to it as you need it. There are a number of factors to consider when you're organizing the layout and storage of your workshop.

# KNIFEMAKING

### *Work Bench/Counter*

In most cases, it's best to have two or more workbenches or counters. You'll want to have a large enough work area that you can work comfortably on without having to put tools on the floor or feel cramped. You'll want the tools you use all the time to be stored near this counter. This will be where you'll be doing much of the work as you make a knife.

A workbench can be made as simply as placing a thick plywood panel across two sawhorses. The nice thing about this kind of workbench is that it's quick to set up, and it's also something that can be easily broken down and stored. Since you'll want to have two workbenches, you can also use this portable model for a second workspace.

## *Tool Storage*

You're going to need several places for storing tools and other supplies. It likely won't be enough to simply utilize cabinets and shelves for this purpose. The first step in this process is to think about how you want to have your tools organized.

You might want to organize them by tool type or perhaps by the order of use in a project. Whatever kind of system you choose, you'll want it to be flexible as you're likely to acquire more tools through the years.

A great way to store tools is to utilize pegboard. You can use hooks to suspend tools, and that way, you can also see the tools so you can quickly find the one you need. You can also utilize a wall-mounted toolbox using the pegboard. Alternatively, you could mount the toolbox on the wall.

Another useful way to store tools is to utilize a rolling mechanic's toolbox. That will allow you to move around the workshop easily with your tools in tow. It also lets you organize a variety of both large and small tools.

## *Extra Materials*

On most if not all projects, you'll end up with some leftover materials. These could be handle or sheath design elements, scrap metal, or other types of leftovers from various projects. It's helpful to keep those around because you might be able to use them on other projects, but you have to be able to find it when you're ready to use it.

You could use small cabinets for this kind of purpose, particularly if the cabinets have drawers. Be sure to label everything so that you can find what you're looking for easily. You can also use open shelves for storing those materials that are bulkier.

**Light and Power**

Just like with space, you can never have too much light or too many electrical outlets. There are many ways you can spend a lot of money on light and power, but if you're on a budget, these options are for you.

For light, you can wire several inexpensive, keyless lamp holders to the ceiling. You can then use 60-watt equivalent LED bulbs to give you the light you need. You can also make good use of numerous reflector lamps for putting more light on a specific task.

To accommodate your lighting needs and your electric-powered equipment, you'll need several strategically located outlets so that you can plug in the various large and small pieces of equipment you need for knifemaking.

It can be helpful to upgrade to 20-amp circuits rather than 15-amp which are standard. The 20-amp circuits require 12-gauge wire in place of the heavier 14-gauge. By using the 20-amp circuits, you won't have to make nearly as many trips to the breaker panel.

It's also very important that the outlets be GFCI protected. GFCI stands for ground-fault circuit interrupter, and this is a type of fast-acting circuit breaker that is designed to shut off the electricity if it detects a ground fault. Ground faults are the most common type of electrical shock hazards. In most areas, GFCI protected outlets are required by the municipal codes.

**Small Equipment Storage**

While many of your tools can be stored on a pegboard where you can easily see them, you'll also need to store smaller equipment. Clear bins that you can see-through are great for this purpose. You can put wood, files, and other small parts or equipment in these. You can also easily label the bins so you can easily find what you need.

For storing blades in progress, the magnetic metal strips mounted to the wall over your workbench work great for this purpose. That will help you keep your projects in process organized so you'll know exactly what you need to do for each one.

**Large Equipment Storage and Considerations**

You'll have several pieces of larger equipment that will also require storage. The consideration for where to put these also depends on the location of electrical outlets. You'll want them to be placed where you don't have to move them to be able to use them. Make sure they're located near an appropriate electrical outlet so they can be easily plugged in for use.

One of the larger pieces of equipment will be your heat-treating oven. You'll want it to be located in a place that is away from anything flammable, but you'll also want it located where you can easily access the burning chamber as well as the source of heat. You'll need to replace propane tanks so you want those to be easily accessible.

You'll probably also want enough space around large equipment so that you can access all sides. That will give you more space in which you can maneuver.

### Other Workshop Considerations

There are a couple of other considerations to think about when putting together your knifemaking workshop. Because of the nature of the work you'll be doing, you'll want to have certain features to keep the shop in good shape and to keep you comfortable.

- **The Floor**: Because you're working with metal and fire, you'll want the floor to be hard, impervious, and durable. You want it to be able to withstand sparks and metal dropping on it as well as possibly other hazards. You also want to be able to mop up messes easily without having to worry about any scratches or dents.

- For these reasons, you'll probably want something like polished concrete. It can take having things dropped on it, it's easy to clean, and it's fireproof.

- **Hood**: You'll want to have a hood for your forge to vent the fumes. You can also make your forge more aesthetically pleasing by using something like wood paneling on the walls and a facade of river rock around the base.

- **Functional Layout**: You want to organize the layout of your workshop according to specific work areas, and that will also dictate where certain equipment is stored. Here are some work area ideas and the equipment stored in each:

- *Dust Work Area*: This should be a separate room that has window fans, air filters, or other ventilation equipment to improve the air quality. This is where you would store your dust-producing equipment including the surface grinder, belt grinder, vice/angle grinder, and so on.

- *How Work Area*: This will be where you do your forging. Here is where you want to store your forge, heat-treat oven, rolling mill, drill press, anvil, leg vice, welding table, torch, etc.

- *Wet Work Area*: This is where you'll want to have etching tubs, a sink, bluing tubs, and similar equipment. This type of work will require that you get some plumbing done in your workshop. You might also need to think about contaminated waste materials and how you will dispose of something like contaminated water.

- *Machining Area*: This is where you will store your drill press, milling machine, chop saw, bandsaw, and other similar types of equipment.

- *Finishing Area*: This is where you keep things like shop rolls, files, needle files and foredom. This can be as simple as a finishing bench.

- *Office*: It might also be practical to have an office area where you can keep important information on your equipment as well as keep track of costs and any sales you might be making. If your workshop is separate from your house, you might also consider putting in a bathroom near your office so you don't have to keep running between the house and the shop.

The work areas don't all have to be separate rooms.

Each area can simply be divided by a work bench dedicated to that specific area. The dust room and office are the only two areas that might require a separate room.

How you design your workshop depends on a number of factors. In the beginning, you may just be using your garage as a work area, but as you get more experienced, you may want to design your own workshop. The most important consideration is that it be something that suits your style for working. It should be organized in a way that makes sense to you and makes your hobby more enjoyable.

## Chapter Summary

In this chapter, we've discussed the basics about setting up your knifemaking workshop. Specifically, we've covered the following topics:

- The location of your workshop;
- The size of your workshop;
- Storage of tools and other equipment;
- The organizational layout of your workshop;
- Electrical and plumbing considerations for your workshop.

In the next chapter you will learn about how to design a knife.

# CHAPTER FOUR

# HOW TO DESIGN YOUR KNIFE

Before you can design the knife you want to make, you need to be familiar with the different kinds of knives. Some people might think that a blade is a blade, but that's not true. There are knives with different angles and shapes that are designed for specific tasks, and they are designed that way because that is the most efficient shape to get the job done.

Before we can discuss the specific shapes of different knives, it's best to begin with the basics. The following discusses the different parts of a knife.

**Parts of a Knife**

# PARTS OF A KNIFE

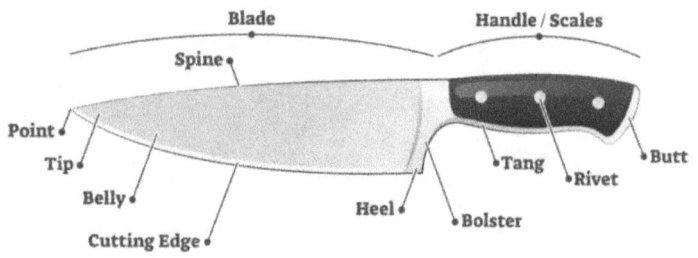

If you're going to design and make a knife, you'll need to know the various parts and their importance. Let's start with the most well-known part of the knife.

- *The Point*: This is the business end of the knife blade. It tapers to a point, which is what gives it its name. There are different shapes to the point, and we'll discuss those shortly, but the importance of the point is that it is what starts making a hole in something, or scores something, or is used to hold something in place, or even to stab something.

- *The Edge*: This is the working part of the knife, and it, too, can have different shapes depending on what the knife's intended use. An edge might be, for example, a V-shape or it could have a convex form.

It could be serrated or it might have multiple bevels. It all depends on the function of the knife.

- A serrated knife has an edge that allows it to be used like a saw or for cutting through tough materials whereas, a knife with a V-shaped edge is more appropriate for chopping. Hollow-grind edges are found most often on chef's knives, and are great for slicing and boning, but this type of edge is also found on pocket knives.

- Flat grind edges are those kinds of edges found on meat cleavers, axes, and machetes. Chisel point edges are typically found on tools whereas convex and compound grind edges are kind of a mix between hollow grind edges and flat grinds, and they are also found on many kitchen knives.

- It's also possible to have a combination on the same blade. Half of the blade might be a hollow grind whereas the other half might be a serrated edge. This is one common combination.

- *The Tip*: This is the very end of the edge, and it is used for delicate cutting.

- *The Heel*: This is the lower part of the blade that is close to where the blade meets the handle, an area called the bolster.

- *The Bolster*: The bolster is the crosspiece that is located where the handle and the blade meet. Its purpose is to protect your fingers. In a knife fight, it could protect your fingers from the opposing blade, and in the kitchen, it can protect your fingers from sliding down onto the edge of the blade when they get slippery.

- *The Spine*: This is the back of the blade if it is a single-edged blade and the middle of the blade if it is a double-edged knife. It's the thickest part of the knife, and it is responsible for giving strength to the edge. In other words, the thicker the spine, the stronger the edge. But, that's not all the spine does. It also affects the balance of the knife.

- Knives where the blade is heavier are better for chopping, but not so great for delicate slicing. Knives where the handle is heavier are perfect for delicate slicing, but they're weak as chopping knives. The spine is what determines whether the knife is blade-heavy or handle-heavy.

- A spine can also have a little texture near the handle at about the last inch. This is referred to as 'jimping' and it allows you to use your thumb at the back of the blade so you have more control when you're making those delicate cuts.

- *Scales*: This is the handle of the knife. The scales can be made from different materials including things like abalone, turquoise, plastic, rubber, wood, leather, micarta, or various polymers. The handle can also be designed with finger grooves if that will help with its use. The design of the handle is important because it affects the ease with which the knife can be used to do something.

- *Tang*: The tang is the metal end of the blade that attaches to the handle. It is not sharpened, and it can be a full-tang, which means the metal extends the full length of the scales, or it can be a partial tang, which means it only extends part of the way into the scales. Knives that are full-tang can withstand much more force applied to the blade, and this is the preferred style for most knives. Folding knives are the one exception to that since they can't be full-tang because they fold.

- *Handle Fasteners*: These hold the scales to the tang, and can be rivets or screws. Rivets are more common because they are less expensive and don't require much maintenance. The problem is that if they loosen up or you want to change them, they are more difficult to remove.

  Screws are easier to remove if you want to change something about the handle and for complete cleaning, but you have to check them periodically and tighten them regularly. They often loosen with use, but you can prevent that by removing them and coating them with Lock-Tite or a similar type of adhesive product.

  Cheap knives will not have fasteners. Instead, the scales will be attached to the tang with epoxy. This is fine if it's just a knife for display, but if you're going to be using it, the handle will fail quickly using this method.

# KNIFEMAKING

- ***Butt.*** This is the back end of the knife.

Now that you have a better understanding about the parts of a knife, it will be easier to discuss the different knife shapes. There are many different possibilities, but here we'll stick to the more common shapes.

There is no one type of knife that can do it all, and more than one knife can work well for the same task. But, if you have a good understanding of the reason behind the shape, then you'll have a better idea how to design the knife you want to make.

## Common Knife Shapes

The following are some of the most common knife shapes. This is by no means an exhaustive list, but you are likely familiar with most of these kinds of knives.

### 1. *Clip Point*

This knife is characterized by a spine that appears to have been clipped off in the front section. That typically produces a concave area that slopes downward from the spine to the point of the blade. This type of knife is great for tasks that require precision cutting.

## 2. *Drop Point*

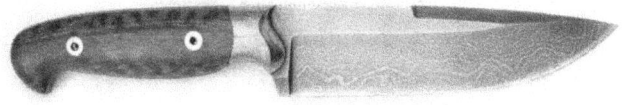

This blade has a convex spine that curves downward from the handle to the point. It's a very common blade shape because its point is more easily controlled, and it has a bigger 'belly' for slicing. These are great general purpose knives that many hunters love.

## KNIFEMAKING

### *3. Gut Hook*

This knife has a small, sharpened hook that interrupts the spine as it curves toward the point. It really has one use: field dressing wild game. Hunters use the hook to cut through an animal's skin so that the tissues under the skin are not damaged. The hook is really more of a feature on the blade than the shape of the blade itself.

### *4. Hawkbill / Talon*

# KNIFEMAKING

This knife is so-named because it kind of looks like a hawk's bill or talon. The spine and the edge both curve downward in the same direction until they come to a point. The edge cuts efficiently then when the knife is pulled back in the direction of the handle, as occurs frequently when doing certain utilitarian tasks like cutting carpet or pruning vegetation.

## 5. *Needle Point*

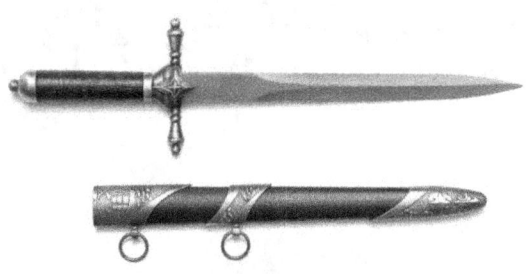

As the name suggests, this is a blade where both edges taper sharply from the handle to the point. This knife is designed for piercing and penetrating, making it a great knife for fighting and stabbing. Because of its narrow shape, however, it is much more fragile than similar blades.

## 6. *Normal / Straight Back*

This blade has a straight spine as the name suggests. The edge curves up to meet the tip. The spine is long and makes for a heavy blade which makes this an ideal knife for chopping and slicing. The long, unsharpened back can help users get more force by applying pressure to this area.

7. *Sheepsfoot*

This blade has a straight edge with a spine that curves down to meet the edge at the point. It's designed for slicing, but also for minimizing the possibility of accidentally piercing your hand with the point. It gets its name because it was originally used for trimming the hooves of sheep, but today it's a very handy rescue tool too!

## 8. Spear Point

This is a symmetrical blade that has a point which is in line with the center of the knife. That makes it a stronger blade than the needle point, and it's also very good for thrusting like a spear. These can be made with either one or two sharp edges, and they are common blades for daggers and throwing knives.

## 9. Spey Point

This blade has a mostly flat edge until it gets close to the tip. Then, the edge curves up to meet the point. The spine is also mostly flat until it angles down to meet the point. That creates a short belly and a broad tip to prevent accidental piercing. These kinds of blades were originally used to neuter animals on farms, but they have become common trapper blades that hunters just love as well!

## *10. Tanto*

This blade was inspired by the short swords that were used by Samurai in feudal Japan. The blade angles up to meet the point rather than curving up. That angular edge makes for a stronger and more prominent point. Because it is more robust and the tip is durable, this is a good knife for piercing tough objects. It doesn't work as well for slicing, however.

# KNIFEMAKING

## *11. Trailing Point*

With a trailing point blade, the spine will curve up to a point that is higher than the handle. That gives it an oversized belly which makes it good for slicing, filleting, and skinning.

## *12. Wharncliffe*

This blade has a straight edge and a curved spine like the sheepsfoot, but the difference is that the curve of the spine extends gradually from the handle all the way to the tip. That makes it ideal for slicing as it also minimizes the possibility of an accidental puncture.

### Fixed Blade versus Folding Blade

One other thing to consider when designing a knife is whether or not it will be a fixed blade knife. There are fixed blade knives and folding blade knives. Fixed blade knives are made for people who really intend to use their knives hard. They are great for use in a kitchen or as general outdoor knives, including in situations such as field-dressing, hunting, filleting, in combat, and diving. They are simply stronger than folding knives and a lot tougher.

The only reason you might consider making a folding knife is if there are considerations for storage, concealment, or transport that require something which can be folded up. Otherwise, folding knives will only be used for light duty.

When making a fixed blade knife, another consideration is whether it will be full-tang or partial tang. Full-tang knives are basically a solid piece of steel, which makes them much stronger. If you're going to put your knife to some serious use, you'll likely want a fixed blade, full-tang knife.

### What's Next?

Once you've decided on the basic shape and type of knife you want to make, now it's time to create the design you'll use to make it. There are some minor design features you'll want to consider like decorative items for the handle, but for the most part, you're ready to create the design.

The first step is to decide what you want the knife to do; what is its intended purpose? Do you want it to chop mostly or cut or piece? What are you designing it to do? The next thing to do is to draw the design, or if you're more technologically savvy, you might use a computer program. If that's not you, then some graph paper and mechanical pencils will do the trick. You want to be able to see how the knife will look proportionally.

Once you have the drawing done—perfectly with every line and curve just like you want it—now you want to make the pattern. This basically involves transferring what you drew onto something more rigid, more substantial than simply paper. Be sure to make copies first so that you don't lose your original design.

When you choose a material for this working model, you want it to be something that is easy to work with like a thin, mild steel or wood. The idea is that you want to make a prototype of the knife you'll eventually make out of steel. You can trace your drawing onto this material with a dark pen and then cut it out of the material.

Most of the time, this is when you realize the knife isn't balanced like you want it, or maybe the guard is too small or the handle is too thick. This is where you can then use a grinder to keep adjusting it until it is perfect for what you want. You might even have to start all over again to get it just right, but you don't want to become discouraged. Even if you have to let it sit for a few days and think about the design, you want to make sure you've got it exactly right. That will pay off in the end and save you a lot of time.

If you just feel like drawing your knife design is more than you want to do, there are free knife designs available on the internet. They are available in printable formats so you don't have to bother with the actual drawing of the design. These are, however, mostly considered to be a starting point for your project. You will need (and want) to add your own style to the designs, but they are suitable for transferring them to steel, wood, or polycarbonate to make your pattern.

**Computer Programs for Knife Designing**

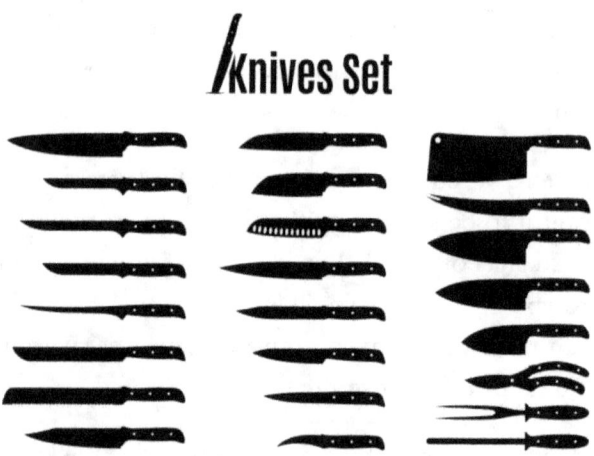

For designing your knife using a computer program, you'll need a graphics design program that supports both 2D and 3D editing. That will give you the most flexibility for your designs. Here are several that work really well for this purpose.

### Adobe Illustrator CC

This program is used by many professional graphic designers, and in fact, it's their preferred program. With this program, you can do anything you can think of related to the design of your knife. You can use free-hand drawing tools or you can select shapes that are based on precise measurements.

This program's professional graphics capabilities mean you are only limited by your imagination, and you'll have all the online tutorials you'll need to learn how to use it. You can also test it out for free for seven days, and it's compatible with the other Adobe products like Photoshop.

### Adobe Photoshop

This is similar to Adobe Illustrator, and in fact, is nearly identical in its capacity for creating designs. The only real difference is that Photoshop focuses more on the editing and image doctoring aspects of graphic design than the design itself.

It's still good for designing, however, since it has all the tools you need for that. What's more, anything you create in Photoshop can be imported into Illustrator to put on the finishing touches. It's also true that this program has been around for a long time, and you've probably heard of it. Like Illustrator, you can also test it out for free for 7 days.

## Autodesk Inventor

This program has a long history of being really good at 3D design, and it's a simple program to use for product design, rendering, and simulation. Moreover, it can create everything from really complex machinery to something as relatively simple as a kitchen knife. It comes with several presets that mean you don't actually have to start from scratch.

It's also one of the easiest Autodesk tools to use so you have a short learning curve, and it's great for manufacturing parts. It also offers animation that allows you to see all sides of the object, and it gives annotated exploded views.

## Autodesk Fusion 360

This is one of the best integrated CAD and design software programs out there. It's great for designing knives because it's intuitive interface picks up on what you're doing and helps you out. It's able to do that because, relatively speaking, designing a knife is simple. What's even better is that this software is free for home users.

## CorelDraw Graphics Suite

This is composed of seven programs that give you everything you will ever need to design anything, including a knife. It contains the following programs:

- CorelDRAW
- Corel PHOTO-PAINT

- Corel Font Manager
- PowerTRACE
- CorelDRAW.app
- CAPTURE
- AfterShot 3 HDR

The first two programs by themselves are sufficient for you to design a knife, but since you can get all seven programs for a good price, you might as well take advantage of that.

Knife design software is really helpful for serious knife craftsmen and hobbyists, and it's a great way to create your unique designs without having to worry about making mistakes. It's also an easy way to modify designs. These software programs all are great for helping you as a knifemaker to design your products with ease and efficiency.

## Chapter Summary

In this chapter, we've discussed how to design your knife. Specifically, we've discussed the following topics:

- The parts of a knife;
- The common shapes of knives;
- Folding versus fixed knives;
- Making your knife prototype
- Computer programs for designing your knife

In the next chapter you will learn about the different kinds of steel and how to choose which one to use for your knife.

KNIFEMAKING

# CHAPTER FIVE

# CHOOSING YOUR STEEL

The choice of which type of steel to use for your blade is one of the most important parts of making a knife. The choice of metal will depend in part on the type of knife you're making as well as budgetary constraints and a few other concerns. To begin, let's discuss a few basic facts about steel.

### What is a Good Steel for Making Knives?

The ideal metal for your project depends on what you plan to use your knife for. Different types of knives are subjected to a variety of different forces. For example, hatchets and machetes need to be designed to withstand significant impacts, and for those, you'll want a stronger metal that won't break when subjected to these forces.

If you're making a finer knife that's designed to do more delicate cutting, you'll certainly want something strong and hard, but it's not going to be subjected to impacts like the machete, so it doesn't have to be as tough.

It is the carbon content that plays a big role in determining the hardness, strength, and toughness of the knife you're making. With a higher carbon content, the metal will be harder and stronger. That's because the carbon helps to hold the iron atoms in place. More is not necessarily better, however, as too much carbon will make the metal brittle, and you risk fracturing the blade upon impact.

In general, you want the knife you're making to have just the right amount of carbon as well as other alloys to be able to perform the task it was made to do without risking breaking it or other types of damage.

## All About Steel—The Basics

Before we discuss the type of steel you'll want to use for the knife you're making, let's talk a little more about steel itself. Steel is a combination of carbon and iron, although it is true that steel also contains small amounts of other elements such as manganese, sulfur, silicon, and phosphorus. If there's nothing else in it, this is referred to as plain carbon steel.

For some knife blades, however, the steel is enhanced with some additional elements. This is referred to as alloy steels, and these additional elements are what give different types of steel their unique properties. For example, if alloy steels have anti-corrosion elements added to them, this is called stainless steel, and it is this steel that is most often used to make knife blades. That makes sense because most knives are exposed to certain elements, like water, that promote corrosion.

To make alloyed steel, you start by melting the steel in your furnace or oven, and then you add the appropriate alloying additives. Once that is done, you can pour the molten steel into a mold, which is called an ingot. After the ingot solidifies, you can then process that in a mill into the shape and size you desire.

## Properties of Steel

When you're selecting steel, you want to consider the application for the knife you're making and the properties of the steel you're considering. This includes factors like how easy it is to manufacture. If it's very difficult to make a particular steel, then it's not really practical to use.

The properties you'll look at also include the alloys that you want to add as well as the method for doing that. Knife blade steel has the following important properties:

- **Strength**: This is referring to the ability of the steel to resist the forces that will be applied to the blade.

- **Hardness**: There is a scale, called the Rockwell Scale, that is used to measure the hardness of steel. What it's measuring is the ability of the steel to resist permanent deformation as a result of the forces to which it is subjected.

- **Hardenability**: This term refers to the ability of the steel to be hardened, which is achieved with the heat-treating process.

- **Toughness**: While many of these terms seem similar, they are actually referring to different properties of the steel. The toughness refers to the ability of the steel to absorb energy before it would break. The more energy it can absorb without breaking, the tougher the blade.

- **Ductility**: This is referring to the ability of the steel to flex or bend without breaking. The more ductile the steel, the less likely it is to break.

- **Initial Sharpness**: This refers to how sharp the blade is "out of the box," so to speak. That means its initial sharpness.

- **Edge Retention**: While the initial sharpness is one measure of quality, it's also important to know how long the steel blade will hold an edge before it needs to be resharpened. That's what edge retention means. If your blade needs to be resharpened frequently, it doesn't have a good edge retention.

- **Wear Resistance**: This is referring to the ability of the steel to resist wear and tear while it's being used. If it ends up with small chips in the edge, its wear resistance isn't very good.

- **Corrosion Resistance**: This is referencing the blade's ability to resist deterioration due to exposure to environmental conditions.

- **Manufacturability**: As suggested above, this is referring to how easy it is to make the steel. What is the ease with which it can be machined, blanked, ground, and heat-treated to produce a blade?

Now that you have a better understanding of the properties of steel, let's move on to a discussion of the types of steel.

# KNIFEMAKING

## Steel Nomenclature

The terms used to describe steel reference its properties and are derived from the internal structure of metals. When you heat and cool the steel, its internal structure does undergo significant changes. In accordance with those structural changes, different classes of steel are given names, such as Austenite and Martensite. Martensite, for example, is an extremely hard structure that is formed through rapidly cooling certain types of steel during the heat-treating process. There are five main classes of stainless steel. They are as follows:

## 1. Austenitic Stainless Steel

This is the largest family of stainless steels, and it makes up approximately two-thirds of all stainless steel production. This type of steel possesses what is called an austenitic microstructure which is achieved by using sufficient amounts of nickel and/or manganese combined with nitrogen in order to create the microstructure and maintain it through all temperature ranges, from the cryogenic region to the melting point.

This process means that Austenitic stainless steels are not able to be hardened by heat-treating since that won't result in changes to their structure. These types of steels are divided into sub-groups called the 200 series and the 300 series.

The 200 series uses chromium-manganese-nickel alloys that maximize the manganese and nitrogen and minimize the nickel. The added nitrogen gives the steel a 50% higher yield strength than the 300 series.

The 300 series use chromium-nickel alloys that provide a greater resistance to acids and localized corrosion due to chloride ions. These kinds of steels are able to avoid problems with corrosion caused by welding.

## 2. Ferritic Stainless Steels

These types of steels have a ferrite microstructure like carbon steel. They contain very little or even no nickel and between 10.5 and 27 percent chromium. Like the Austenite steels, this microstructure is present through all temperature ranges, and so, these steels are not able to be hardened by heat-treating. Additionally, these kinds of steels are magnetic.

Because they don't have much, if any, nickel, these stainless steels are less expensive and present in several different kinds of products including automobile exhaust pipes, building components, and power plates.

## 3. Martensitic Stainless Steels

This kind of steel is commonly used in kitchen knives. It has a broad range of properties and many varied purposes. They are magnetic, but they are not as resistant to corrosion as the Ferritic and Austenitic steels. That's because they have a lower chromium content. There are four categories of Martensitic steels:

- Fe-Cr-C grades, which were the first used and are commonly found in engineering and wear-resistant applications.

- Fe-Cr-Ni-C grades, in which some of the carbon is replaced with nickel. These are tougher and more resistant to corrosion. These have good casting properties as well as weldability and resistance to cavitation erosion. The latter is caused when small vapor-filled cavities form in the steel due to rapid changes in pressure.

- Precipitation hardening grades, which are the best known of these steels. They combine martensitic hardening with precipitation hardening (see below). That results in a higher strength and good toughness, which makes these steels suitable for aerospace applications.

- Creep-resisting grades, which add small amounts of niobium, vanadium, boron, and cobalt to increase strength. It also makes them more creep resistant. This refers to the tendency of solid materials like steel to deform slowly over time (creep) when exposed to persistent mechanical stresses.

Martensitic steels are heat-treatable, which provides them with better mechanical properties. This is done in three stages that begin with heating the steel to between 1,800 and 1,920 degrees Fahrenheit. The heating is then followed by quenching where the Austenite metal formed by the heating is rapidly cooled, thereby transforming the Austenite into Martensite. The resulting Martensite is too brittle at this point for most applications. It is then tempered by heating to around 932 degrees Fahrenheit; it is held at that temperature and then allowed to air cool. This will decrease both yield and tensile strength, but it increases impact resistance.

Recent developments in the production of Martensitic stainless steel includes replacing the carbon with nitrogen. When the nitrogen is melted under high pressure, it results in an increase in hardness and strength combined with more resistance to corrosion. This is, however, an expensive process.

### 4. Duplex Stainless Steel

These stainless steels are a mixture of Austenite and Ferrite microstructures. The ideal ratio is a 50:50 mix, but the commercial alloys often have ratios of 40:60. These steels have higher chromium percentages (19 - 32 percent), and they have more molybdenum (as much as 5 percent). They have lower nickel content than Austenite steels. This combination results in approximately twice the yield strength as compared to Austenitic stainless steel. They are also more resistant to chloride stress corrosion.

These steels are divided into three sub-groups: lean duplex, standard duplex, and super duplex. The duplex steels overall have a lower alloy content than the Austenitic grades, and that makes them more cost effective. These steels are used in the pulp and paper industry and the oil and gas industry. The latter prefers more corrosion-resistant grades, which has led to the development of the super and hyper duplex grades. You'll find the lean duplex grade used for structural application in the construction industry.

## 5. Precipitation Hardening Stainless Steels

Precipitation hardening is a heat-treating technique that results in an increase in yield strength. It relies on changes in the solubility of solids as the temperature increases, which produces fine particles that impede the movement of defects in the crystal lattice of the metal's microstructure. These defects aid with plasticity, which helps harden the material. To achieve the precipitation of the solid particles, the alloys of these steels have to be kept at an elevated temperature for hours in a process referred to as aging.

This type of heat treatment makes the steels more resistant to corrosion than comparable Austenitic steels. Additionally, they can be hardened to higher strength levels than other Martensitic grades. There are three types of these steels: Martensitic, Semi-Austenitic, and Austenitic.

The stainless steels used for making blades mainly involve Martensitic stainless steels, particularly those blades made for the cutlery industry.

# KNIFEMAKING

## Alloy Additions

An important part of stainless steel are the alloys that are added to create certain properties. The following are common alloys along with a description of how they affect steel properties.

- Carbon: This is already present in plain carbon steels, but you can increase the amount to increase hardness. You just have to be careful not to increase it too much or the metal will be brittle.

- Chromium: This additive will help improve the hardness, wear resistance, and corrosion resistance. It's one of the main additions of Martensitic stainless steels.

- Molybdenum: This also improves the hardness as well as the tensile strength, and corrosion resistance, particularly pitting.

- Nickel: This improves toughness, hardness, and corrosion resistance. It is the main element in Austenitic stainless steels, which are often used for dive knives.

- Vanadium: This improves hardness and it promotes fine grains that help make the steel stronger and more resistant to wear and tear. In general, you want fine grain structures in steel.

**Commonly Used Steel Types**

Within each class of stainless steel, there are different types of steel. Each type is produced with a precise recipe which will ensure consistency in the steel properties. The recipes are called specifications since they specify the amount of the alloy additions. These types are named using numbers. For example, Martensitic steels include Type 410, 420, and 425, among others.

Here are the main types of steels used in making blades:

**S30V:** This type of steel is primarily used by the cutlery industry. It contains higher levels of carbon and vanadium which provide the steel with better edge-retention and resistance to abrasion. It is considered the best blade steel available today for the following reasons:

- Better edge retention
- Better ductility
- Good hardness—that means within the ideal range of Rc 59.5 - 61
- Good resistance to corrosion
- Very high levels of carbon and vanadium

The recipe for S30V is as follows:

- Carbon: 1.45 percent
- Chromium: 14.0 percent
- Vanadium: 4.0 percent
- Molybdenum: 2.0 percent

**BG-42**: This is a proprietary alloy of Timken Latrobe Steel. It is a Martensitic stainless steel used in the aerospace industry, but it is well-suited for blades because of its high Rockwell hardness (Rc 61 - 62). That makes it particularly suitable for blades that are subjected to extreme forces. Its qualities include the following:

- Good edge retention
- High strength

- Rockwell Rc of 61 to 62
- Fair resistance to corrosion
- Vanadium is one of the ingredients, which improves hardenability and fine grain structure

The recipe is as follows:

- Carbon: 1.15 percent
- Silicon: 0.3 percent
- Chromium: 13.5 to 14.5 percent
- Molybdenum: 4 percent
- Vanadium: 1.2 percent

**154CM**: This is a high carbon stainless steel that also includes molybdenum. That results in better edge retention, particularly for most standard cutlery steels. It's a great choice for those blades that will be doing heavier cutting. The qualities include the following:

- Good edge retention
- Rockwell Rc 60 to 61
- Good toughness if double tempered
- Fair corrosion resistance
- More affordable than BG-42 or S30V

The recipe is as follows:

- Carbon: 1.05 percent
- Silicon: 0.35 percent
- Chromium: 13.5 to 14.0 percent
- Molybdenum: 4.0 percent

**420HC**: This is a higher carbon version of the Martensitic stainless steel Type 420. With the higher carbon content in combination with a high chromium content, blades made from this steel have good edge retention and wear resistance. It produces a great general purpose blade when properly heat-treated. The qualities include the following:

- Good edge retention
- Resharpens well
- Rockwell Rc 58
- Good toughness
- Great corrosion resistance
- Makes an excellent standard knife steel

The recipe is as follows:

- Carbon: 0.40 - 0.50 percent
- Nickel: 0.50 percent

- Silicon: 0.60 percent
- Chromium: 12.0 to 14.0 percent
- Manganese: 1.0 percent

**420J2**: This steel has a lower carbon content, but it's a good general purpose stainless steel. It has a fair level of hardness and corrosion resistance, but it is very easy to resharpen. It is well-suited for blades that are made for light to medium uses and more routine applications. Its qualities are the following:

- Resharpens very well
- Rockwell Rc 56 - 58
- Good corrosion resistance
- Good manufacturability

The recipe is as follows:

- Carbon: 0.36 to 0.45 percent
- Nickel: 0.60 percent
- Silicon: 0.60 percent
- Chromium: 12.00 - 14.00 percent
- Manganese: 0.80 percent

**17-7 PH**: This stainless steel is precipitation-hardened and contains chromium, nickel, and aluminum alloys. That combination is great for applications that require a lot of strength and that require good resistance to salt-water corrosion. This steel is a compromise between Martensitic steels that are heat-treatable and Austenitic steels that are not, and that's due to the high content of chromium, nickel, and aluminum. This steel has the following qualities:

- Moderate edge retention
- Very good toughness
- Excellent resistance to corrosion
- Rockwell Rc 54 – 56

The recipe is as follows:

- Carbon: 0.07 percent
- Vanadium: trace amount
- Chromium: 17.00 percent
- Molybdenum: trace amount
- Nickel: 7.0 percent
- Aluminum: 1.25 percent

A comparison of these steels gives the following results with 4 being best, 3 being better, 2 being good, and 1 being fair.

| Steel Type | Edge Retention | Ease of Resharpening | Corrosion Resistance |
|---|---|---|---|
| S30V | 4 | 3 | 2 |
| BG42 | 3 | 2 | 2 |
| 154CM | 3 | 2 | 2 |
| 420HC | 2 | 3 | 3 |
| 420J2 | 2 | 3 | 2 |
| 17-7PH | 1 | 4 | 4 |

## Other Steels for Knifemaking

While the above listed steels are some of the best, there are other steels used for knifemaking as well. Here's a list of some of the more commonly used steels:

**AUS-8**: This steel is also referred to as 8A. This steel has a high carbon, low chromium content, and it has been shown to be a very good compromise between toughness, edge retention, resistance to corrosion, and strength.

**ATS-34**: This stainless steel is premium grade, and it is used by custom knifemakers and those factories that produce higher quality knives. It is a Japanese steel that produces high quality blades.

**CPM-T440V**: This is often called the 'super steel,' because it outlasts every other stainless steel on the market today. The drawback is that it is harder to resharpen, but that's because its edge retention is unprecedented, so you don't have to sharpen it very frequently. It is used by custom knifemakers, and it's quickly becoming a favorite of high-end knife factories.

**San Mai III**: In Japanese, this translates as 'three layers.' It was so-named for its use to make traditional laminated blades that are used for Japanese swords and daggers. The lamination allows different grades of steel to be combined in the making of a single blade. An easy way to visualize that is to imagine a sandwich. In the center is a hard, high carbon steel, and on either side (the bread of the sandwich) are lower-carbon, tough panels. The edge is typically very hard so that edge retention is good, but the rest of the blade is not as hard since that would predispose it to damage during battles. The body is extremely tough so that it can withstand lateral stresses and impacts. Normally, that body toughness would prevent the edge from retaining its sharpness, but because the middle part of the laminated layers is a hard, high carbon steel, the edge lasts longer even as the sides are flexible.

**VG-1 Stainless Steel**: This steel type has been tested and the results show it has the greatest performance increases in edge retention, point strength, shock, sharpness, and overall strength. It provides previously unavailable superior performance in stainless steel blades.

**4116 Krupp Stainless Steel**: This is a German-made stainless steel type that is fine-grained and used for hygienic applications, like in medical devices and the pharmaceutical industry. It is also used for food processing and in kitchen cutlery. It has a balance of carbon and chromium which gives it great resistance to corrosion as well as good strength and edge retention. In fact, its edge retention exceeds the 420 and 440 series of stainless steel. It also contains alloys that contribute to grain refinement which increases the strength of the blade and the toughness of the edge. It also makes the edge finer and sharper for more delicate cutting applications.

**1055 Carbon Steel**: This steel falls in between a medium and high content carbon steel. The carbon content is between 0.50 and 0.60 percent. It also contains between 0.60 and 0.90 percent manganese, which is the only other component of the steel. This produces a Rockwell Rc of 60 - 64 depending on the specific carbon content. That makes this one of the toughest steels available, since once it is quenched, it produces a Martensite steel with no excess carbides that would otherwise make higher carbon steels brittle. That makes this steel well-suited for applications that require strength and impact resistance.

**SK-5 High Carbon Steel**: This is the Japanese equivalent of the American 1080 stainless steel. It has a high carbon content between 0.75 and 0.85 percent, and that is combined with manganese at 0.60 to 0.90 percent. When quenched, it produces a hardness level of Rockwell Rc 65. It does have some excess carbide that increases the wear resistance and produces a blade that is well-balanced between toughness and edge holding ability. This steel is typically used for hand tools like chisels and woodcutting saws.

### Where to Acquire Steel

You can actually find steel for making knives easily online and it's not very expensive, either. You can even find it on Amazon.com for between $25 and $140 depending on the thickness and amount you're looking to buy. If you're thinking about turning your knifemaking hobby into a business venture, it's advisable to buy annealed steel. Annealing is a type of heat treatment that reduces hardness and increases ductility, while also eliminating internal stresses. This makes it more malleable for shaping. If, however, you like the idea of recycling metal instead of buying it new, there are other options as well.

# KNIFEMAKING

## Reclaimed Metal

You find a number of second-hand items that contain scrap metal on sites like craigslist.com. You can often find inexpensive washing machines, lawnmowers, and other items containing scrap metal that's useful for making blades. You might even have some old things around your house that you no longer use and can be harvested for scrap metal.

There are a number of scrap pieces of metal that you might have just been waiting to become a knife blade. Not all scrap metal is equal, however, but you might as well experiment with older pieces of steel if you've got them. Older steel also tends to be higher quality as well. Here's a list of possible sources of scrap metal.

- **Suspension springs**: You might not think about these because they're coiled, but a coil is a wrapped piece of metal, so you can unwrap it and make use of it for a blade.

- **Leaf springs**: Leaf springs from an old truck are excellent sources of steel for making a knife blade. You'll need to anneal them to make them more malleable, but they have the benefit of being flat, wide bards of steel, which makes it less work to shape them.

- **Steel cable**: Steel cable is just braided steel, and it can be separated and used for one or more knives depending on the size of the cable you have. If you happen to find an elevator cable, this works great because it's built to stand up to high tension. That means it's got a higher carbon percentage, which is great for making knives.

- **Circular saw blade**: A circular saw blade is great for making a knife blade, and you won't even have to use the entire saw blade. If you find an older blade, that's better, since they are made of extremely hard steel with good edge retention. Newer saw blades have a different chemical makeup, so they're not as strong though they tend to be sharper.

- **Railroad spikes**: These make really unique and scary knives. They are typically made of carbon-rich steel that is stronger, harder, and more durable, since it needs to resist the impacts that come from the hammering when they are first laid on tracks. They won't have great edge retention, but they're definitely strong. What's more, they're a great size for your hand, and the larger tang gives you some room to do a little custom metalwork or engraving that will really make the knife stand out from the crowd.

- **Steel files**: This is one of the most popular scrap metals for making your first steel knife. Older files are great for small, sharp blades that easily fit in your hand. They're made to be extremely hard, which isn't ideal, but if you anneal them to soften the steel, you'll be able to shape it better and then re-harden it. Once that's done, you'll have a versatile blade that is both hard and holds an edge well.

**What to Look for in Scrap Metal**

These are some great ideas for finding scrap metal, but basically if you're looking for scrap metal to make blades, you want to look for things that are regularly put under some kind of stress. The steel used in an item like that will have a higher percentage of carbon which allows it to withstand the strain, but it will also have a low enough percentage of carbon that it won't be brittle. Items like that are perfect for all-purpose knives.

You also want to look for a piece that's similar in size to what you want to make. You can hammer out different shapes, but you have to have enough steel to make the blade you want to make. You can cut down a larger piece of steel, but you can't add more to a small piece.

You also want to perform some easy and basic tests on any scrap metals you're thinking about using to get a basic idea of their hardness, strength, and toughness.

**Testing Scrap Metals**

There are a couple of ways to test scrap metals to make sure they're made out of the quality of steel you want for your blade.

1. **Harden and Break:** You can take a small piece of the metal and heat it up until it loses its magnetism. Then, you quench it in oil to harden it—lots of common metals are oil quenchable. Then, once you've quenched and cooled the piece, you can put it in a vice and hit is with a hammer. If the steel is hardenable, it will break instead of bending. If it bends instead, that means it's either low carbon steel or steel that requires water quenching. So, heat it up again and water quench it. Then let it cool, put it in a vice and hit it again with the hammer. If it still bends rather than breaking, that means it won't work for your knife blade because it won't hold an edge.

2. **Spark Test**: For this test, just take a piece of the steel and touch it with your grinding wheel. Look at the

color and shape of the sparks it produces. No sparks means the metal isn't iron, so that won't work. White sparks indicate titanium content. These are very white and quite luminous. Dark red sparks indicate nickel, cobalt, or tungsten carbide content. Also, the number of forks (divisions) of the spark and the smaller divisions or bursts called sprigs is proportional to the carbon content of the metal. The more carbon, the more sprigs you will see.

3. **Magnetism:** Testing the magnetism will help you identify the alloys or at least narrow down the possibilities.

You want to do these basic, simple tests on any scrap metal you're thinking about using. That way you won't waste your time making a knife from metal that simply won't work for that purpose.

**Scrap Metal Sources**

If you don't have your own lying around, you'll need to find a source for your scrap metal. There are a number of possibilities. You might find some in your immediate neighborhood. If you don't have an old lawnmower you no longer use, perhaps your neighbor does. Often, they're more than happy to share with you and they might also want to learn more about your hobby too.

Local businesses can also be another source of scrap metal. Try asking appliance and auto repair shops if they have scrap metal items that are no longer usable for their purposes. You can take it off their hands so they don't have to worry about disposing of it. There may also be scrap metal you can find in manufacturing facilities, warehouses, hotels, supermarkets, public schools, and even farms.

You'll also want to check the local junkyard, since you're bound to find a variety of items you can use there. as the saying goes, 'one man's trash is another man's treasure.' You can also check construction and renovation sites, as well as dumpsters and dump sites. Finally, you can check at medical facilities for things like old beds, wheelchairs, damaged equipment, wheeled trays, and the like. Of course, these should be disinfected thoroughly before you take them.

**Annealing Steel**

If you need to anneal the steel you get, it's a pretty easy process. Simply heat the steel to approximately 100 degrees Fahrenheit above the critical temperature. Typically that means you're heating to a range of 1450 - 1650 degrees Fahrenheit. When you're done with that, soak it for one hour per each inch of thickness, and then let it cool at a rate no faster than 70 degrees Fahrenheit per hour. You can use dry sand or dry vermiculite to let it cool. These will allow the piece to keep its warmth for longer so it will cool at a slow enough pace. Vermiculite is a soil additive for plants, and it happens to be a great insulator. Sand is also known for its heat retention properties. Make sure both are very pure though. They shouldn't have any mud or roots in the mix. Once you've finished the annealing process, you're ready to make your blade.

# KNIFEMAKING

## Chapter Summary

In this chapter, we've discussed how to choose the steel you'll use for making your blade. Specifically, we've covered the following topics:

- The basics about steel;
- The properties of steel;
- The nomenclature of steel;
- The classes of steel;
- The types of steel;
- Where to acquire steel;
- How to anneal steel.

In the next chapter you will learn about forging your knife.

KNIFEMAKING

# CHAPTER SIX

# FORGING AND HEATING METAL

Now that you've chosen your steel, designed your knife, and gotten the tools you need for making a knife, it's time to forge and shape the metal. We'll discuss the actual knifemaking steps in the next chapter, but in this chapter, we'll cover what you need to be able to forge and heat-treat your blade. For this kind of work, the following are the tools you'll need:

- **Safety Gear**: It's important to remember that you're working with fire, hot metal, and sharp edges. You'll want to protect your skin, hands, and eyes. That means you'll want safety goggles, gloves, and long sleeves to protect your arms. You may also want a mask to cover your mouth and nose since you are burning metal and alloys and there will be fumes. It's also a great idea to have a first aid kit handy, one that includes first aid for burns.

- **Metal Prep Tools**: This includes things like an angle grinder or hacksaw that you can use to cut the metal to size. It also includes fire to anneal the steel if that is something you will need to do.

- **Forge**: You can either purchase or make a heat-treating oven. See below this list for a simple DIY heat-treat oven.

- **Anvil**: This is basically just a big piece of metal that you can use to hammer metal on.

- **Hammer**: This is for shaping the knife into the basic form you want.

- **Tongs**: You can use large pliers, but you'll probably want to have something dedicated to this purpose.

- **Fire Tools**: This includes the quench tub, a hot cutter (the edge of an anvil can work for this purpose as would a hacksaw or angle grinder. You'll also need fuel for the forge.

- **File**: This will help you do more fine shaping and sharpening.

- **Grinder**: This is also something you can use to cut as well as shape the metal.

**Sources of Heat**

There are several different ways you can heat the metal for your knife. You may have heard the various terms oven, kiln, forge, and furnace, but what are the differences between these, and what is right for making knives? Let's take a quick look at each.

**Kiln**

A kiln is an enclosed oven that reaches extremely high temperatures. Because it doesn't melt or subvert the form of what is being heated, it is very suitable for drying out ceramics and clay or for something like adding a layer of glaze. Typically, steel won't need to be heated to the high temperatures that kilns reach, but a kiln could conceivably do double duty if you or someone in your family also likes to make pottery.

### Forges

A forge differs from kilns, ovens, and furnaces in that it is more of an open fire pit, although there are also forging ovens. Forges are used to shape metal while hot. Typically, the metal will be heated in an oven or furnace and then it will be taken to the forging press where it will be shaped. For this reason, you might have both a heat-treat oven as well as a forge.

### Furnaces

Furnaces heat to extreme temperatures, and they can be used for annealing, smelting, or even finishing metal. Usually though, furnaces are used on an industrial scale for large steel projects rather than by knifemaking hobbyists.

### Ovens

There are many different types of ovens, some for domestic use and some for commercial use. Usually, ovens don't reach the kind of extreme temperatures needed for something like pottery, but they are ideal for treating steel. They don't get that hot and they are able to maintain a steady temperature. This enables them to heat the steel throughout.

As a beginning knifemaker, you'll probably want a heat-treating oven and possibly a forge as well. This will allow you to sufficiently heat metal throughout and then proceed to shape it using your forge. Both a heat-treating oven and a forge can be purchased, but you can also make each yourself.

## DIY Heat-Treating Oven

You can always buy a heat-treating oven. They run between approximately $750 and $1000, but if that's not in your budget, you can also make one. There are many different ways to make a heat-treating oven; this is offered as just one example.

The one described here is a simple, but effective furnace that will be suitable for your knifemaking needs. The measurements given are only a guide. You can make the oven any size that suits your needs, but if you try to make it smaller, that will interfere with installing the elements.

# KNIFEMAKING

- Here are the measurements:

- **The casing**: 310 mm wide X 270 mm high X 465 mm deep

- **The internal chamber**: 145 mm wide X 110 mm high X 380 mm deep

This size is good for most sizes of knives that you might make with the possible exception of very large Bowie or camping knives.

***Furnace Body***: You'll need at least 24 fire bricks, which are lightweight, Type 23 insulation bricks. Don't use the hard, heavy fire bricks since these don't insulate well, and you will have difficulty carving the grooves for the heating elements.

For this size of oven, you will need some 20 gauge stainless or mild steel sheets. You can have these cut by guillotine at the steel supplier. You will need these to be perfectly square. Here are what you'll need:

- Two sheets that are 300 mm wide by 460 mm long for the top and bottom of your case;

- Two sheet that are 260 mm wide by 460 mm long for each side of the case;

- Two that are 300 mm wide by 260 mm high for the ends—the back and the front door.

You will also need 5.4 meters of 25 mm by 25 mm by 3 mm thick angle iron and lots of 5 mm pop rivets.

You'll use the angle and sheet steel to make a box on legs. Don't secure the top of the box since you'll need to remove it to install the heating elements and fire bricks.

Once the box is made, put the fire bricks into the case. Work from the center outward, and then you can cut the bricks to fit perfectly. They'll end up being about 35 mm wide on each side. The bricks are easy to cut using a hand saw that you would use on wood. You can also use a hacksaw to trim the bricks and carve the heating element grooves. Make sure that, as you cut your bricks, you number them so that you remember where you should put them.

For the heating elements, you'll need four equally-spaced grooves down each side of the brick. The heating element needs to fit snugly inside these grooves. It will help to cut the grooves so that they're slightly angled inward. That will hold the elements better. You can do that by cutting two parallel cuts using your handsaw and then breaking out the middle section. You can also use the hacksaw blade to shape the bottom of the grooves. You can then take the heating element itself and rub it along the groove to make it smooth.

The elements have to be made from Kanthal wire rated at 13 amp, 3.1 KW, 240 V. You'll need two elements that are 0.270 inches in depth and 34 inches long. It is critical that each element is stretched to a minimum of 60 inches and it should not be stretched more than 140 inches. These elements are designed to function at a maximum temperature of 2300 degrees Fahrenheit. After you have stretched the elements, you can fit them into the grooves, which should be rounded on the ends where they change directions. Think of a horseshoe curve on a mountain. That's how the grooves will appear.

The two elements will be joined together using a 6 mm stainless nut and bolt. The two ends of the elements will be put through the back wall of the furnace fire bricks by securing them with two more 6 mm X 100 mm stainless steel bolts. It is imperative that these bolts do not come into contact with the furnace since that can short out the elements and electrify the metal case. You can make the holes in the back wall about 25 mm in diameter to ensure the bolts are well clear of the metal. You can use something like Tuffnol insulation board to give the bolts something to tighten against.

You will use high temperature insulated wire that is specific to furnaces and kilns to run from the element bolts to the control for the oven. All connections should be covered with insulation before using the oven. You'll then have to connect the wires to an electricity source, but basically, you'll want the same type of control that you would use for your regular cooking oven. You'll need a method to measure the temperature with a K type thermocouple. You can find these at a reasonable price, but make sure they measure up to at least 1100 degrees Celsius, as you'll be heating your stainless steel to those temperatures. You can find programmable controls and thermocouples that will both read and set the temperature.

Once the elements are in place, you can construct the front door using the 25 mm X 25 mm angle iron and stainless steel sheet. The door should have an overall thickness of approximately 50 mm. You'll want it constructed in such a way as to allow you to remove the top of the door to slide the fire bricks into place. You can also affix a 25 mm wide asbestos substitute tape to the face of the door to act as a seal. If you've got a good seal on the door, you'll be better able to reach your desired temperatures, and you won't have as much temperature fluctuation while heating. You can mount the door on simple metal hinges that are riveted to both the door and the side of the furnace.

**DIY Propane Forge**

# KNIFEMAKING

A forge can be easily set up in your workshop, but you do have to think about venting the smoke and fumes it will produce. To make a forge, you will need two things: a box that will hold the heat and a burner to make heat. Let's begin with the burner. For the burner, you will need the following equipment:

- 8" long, 3/4" black pipe nipple
- A 1/2" to 3/4" pipe reducer
- 3" long, 1/8" pipe nipple—this should be either brass or steel
- 1/8" pipe cap—this should be the same material as the pipe nipple above
- 1/8" to 1/4 " NPT brushing that is the same material as above
- 1/4" ball valve
- A 0.040" or 0.045" MIG welding tip
- 3 inches of 1" I.D. pipe
- Five 3/4" long #4 set screws—you'll need three of these sets if you want to mount the 1/8" nipple to the face of the pipe reducer
- Two U-brackets for holding the 1/8" pipe nipple and 4 machine screws of a suitable size for the brackets—this is also needed if you want to mount the nipple to the face of the pipe reducer.

# KNIFEMAKING

For mounting, the pipe reducer will need to be modified slightly to accept the 1/8" pipe nipple which will carry the gas flow. To do that, drill two 7/16" holes in the side of the reducer so that the pipe nipple can pass through the center of the large end. It's also necessary to drill and tap two holds for set screws in the back of the reducer in order to retain the pipe nipple. It is also possible to use pipe hold-down clamps attached to the 1/8" pipe nipple, and for this, you'll need to drill and tap four holds for the clamps to be bolted to the back of the reducer.

You'll also need to modify the 1/8" pipe nipple since it provides the gas flow to the burner and contains the gas metering jet. The simplest way to do this is to drill a #60 wire sized hole in the pipe nipple. While it's more complicated, you might also drill and tap the nipple so that it will accept the MIG-welding-gun tip.

Once you've modified the pipe reducer and pipe nipple, it's pretty easy to bolt the rest of the burner together. Thread the 8" long 3/4" pipe nipple into the 3/4" side of the pipe reducer. Then, insert the 1/8" pipe nipple through the holds (or under the clamps) on the other end of the pipe reducer. If you choose to use the welding tip as a gas jet, install the welding tip at this point. Assemble the pipe cap onto one of the protruding ends of the 1/8" pipe nipple using teflon tape or pipe dope. You can also use the teflon tape or pipe dope to then connect the plumbing to the propane line from your regulator on the other protruding end of the pipe nipple. The plumbing includes the 1/8" to 1/4" NPT brushing and the 1/4" NPT ball valve. With those, the 1/4" propane hose connects the regulator on the propane tank. Be sure to get an older style propane tank connection. The newer ones shut down propane flow if it thinks there is a leak, but it will perceive the flow in this burner as a huge leak, so it will keep shutting you down. That's why you want the older style.

The last thing you need to make in the burner is the cone. This will require some forging, which can be accomplished with an oxyacetylene torch and a rosebud tip, or you might know someone who already has a forge you can use. If that doesn't work either, you can hold off on this step until your forge is ready. To make it, flare one end of the cone to about 1/8" larger than the other, and after it has cooled, drill and tap three screw sets 120 degrees apart to connect it to the burner. You'll want to position this cone until you have the pressure of flame you desire.

Once the burner has been made, you're ready to build the box. A forge is basically a box that's made out of refractory material and steel that contains and supports it. You can use refractory brick that you might find at a ceramics supply or kiln repair store, but if you don't have something like that near you, you can also order it online.

You can make any size of forge, but for knifemaking it really doesn't need to be too big. The width of the forge will be dictated by the length of your brick. If you need something wider, you would have to choose a different refractory material or you could also make an arch with the bricks to span the distance. You can leave the back of the forge open for longer knives, but it might be better to install a window at the back rather than leaving it open, since an open forge loses a lot of heat. If you need it to be open, you can pile extra refractory bricks at the open ends.

The nice thing about using refractory bricks is that they are easy to cut and drill, but are also brittle, so buy a little more material than you think you will need since you might destroy some of it along the way. Before beginning, make sure you have a design that meets your needs and the required layout of the refractory material you're using. Once you know that, it's just a matter of designing the outer support of steel that will hold the refractory material in place. Inside the forge, your refractory material needs to be arranged so that it will support itself. That's why using refractory bricks is a simple way to do this.

Once you've got the box built with its refractory material in place, it's time to combine the burner with the forge. You want the burner to be centrally located, and part of that is determining how to attach it to the frame of the forge. You can use a flat bar bent into a U shape to claim the 3/4" black pile of the burner to the forge frame, for example. You can also simply buy U clamps as well. You'll also need to cut a hole where the burner passes through the refractory material. Fire brick is easily cut with a handsaw.

Once you've successfully attached the burner to the forge, you're ready to fire it up and start forging!

**Choosing the Fuel for Your Forge**

If you're using a forge, you will have to make a choice of fuel for forging. Most of the time, your choice is between propane, coal, or charcoal. The DIY forge above uses propane, but you can build one that uses either coal or charcoal. Here are the benefits and drawbacks of each.

**Propane**: This fuel is clean and readily available. It also burns very hot. In fact, with a propane torch, you can even directly heat metal to the point where you can work it. You can also buy a forge that has an integrated propane heat source, or you can build it into yours.

**Coal**: This is a very hot-burning fuel, and it can easily fit into most forges, but it makes a lot of smoke. For that reason, you'll need proper ventilation in your workshop. Still, if the neighbors see the smoke, they might call the fire department. In some areas, coal is illegal to burn, so check your local laws before choosing this fuel.

**Charcoal**: This is an affordable fuel source, but it doesn't work for everyone. You can make it by burning your own wood, so it's also readily available. The problem is that it doesn't burn very hot, and so, even efficient forges have trouble reaching and maintaining high enough temperatures to forge steel. That makes charcoal the less preferred option, but if it's all you got, then give it a try.

All three fuel sources will need an air intake in order to fan the flames, so that's something to ensure you have on your forge. In the DIY forge above, the open end serves as an air intake. If you go with a different design, however, you may need to specifically create an air intake.

With an oven, a forge, a hammer, and an anvil, you're ready to forge the steel. Remember that your hammer and anvil need to be heat-proof so that the hot metal you'll be bringing them in contact with won't burn. Also, the hammer needs to be heavy enough that it can stand up to steel.

**The Forging Process**

It's important to remember that the red-hot metal you'll be working with can cause third degree burns before you even have a chance to react to the heat. So, take the proper precautions, be careful around the heat, and have a first aid kit handy for any accidents that may occur.

**Managing the Heat**

You want the fire in your oven and/or forge to be going well so that there is a red/orange hot area where you can put the steel. If you already have a straight piece of steel, you won't need to do this next part. If you need to straighten your steel, heat it in the orange hot area and then pound it out straight on the anvil. As the metal cools, reheat it until you have been able to straighten it as desired. One thing to be aware of is that if the metal gets too hot—that means yellow to white hot—it will spark. That's caused by the carbon burning out of it and burning away iron. If that happens, you'll want to cut off the burnt piece and start again. Steel that is not high-carbon steel won't be able to be hardened, and so, you can't use it for a knife blade.

It's important to understand the color changes that occur as you heat the steel. It's great if you have a forge that has a thermostat, and in that case, set it at 2,200 degrees Fahrenheit. To determine the steel's temperature, however, you can use the following color guide.

| Degrees Fahrenheit | Color | Degrees Celsius |
|---|---|---|
| 2000 | Bright Yellow | 1093 |
| 1900 | Dark Yellow | 1038 |
| 1800 | Orange Yellow | 982 |
| 1700 | Orange | 927 |
| 1600 | Orange Red | 871 |
| 1500 | Bright Red | 816 |
| 1400 | Red | 760 |
| 1300 | Medium Red | 704 |
| 1200 | Dull Red | 649 |
| 1100 | Slight Red | 593 |
| 1000 | Very Slight Red, Mostly Grey | 538 |
| 800 | Dark Grey | 427 |
| 575 | Blue | 302 |
| 540 | Dark Purple | 282 |
| 520 | Purple | 271 |
| 500 | Brown/Purple | 260 |
| 480 | Brown | 249 |
| 465 | Dark Straw | 241 |

| 445 | Light Straw | 229 |
| 390 | Faint Straw | 199 |

The reason the steel gives off these colors is that the atoms are so energized they are giving off photons that cause an oxide layer to form on the surface and that reflects color as light. If it's not practical for you to use color to attempt to determine the steel temperature (many people are color blind, for example), you'll need an oven with an accurate thermometer. There are also a few other indicators of steel temperature when you're heating it to harden it.

You might recall that when steel begins to change to Austenite, it loses its magnetism, and that's an indicator of it reaching critical temperature. If you are able to get a type-K thermocouple as recommended for the heat-treating oven above, you can plug that into a digital multimeter and then convert the millivolts to temperature. This can be achieved by passing the thermocouple through a small hole in your gas forge. It works pretty well.

Finally, you can also use tempilstiks. Tempilstiks are basically color-coded crayons that melt within one percent of their temperature rating. They come in a wide range of temperatures that go up to 2,500 degrees Fahrenheit. They are available from blacksmith/forge supply dealers.

## Quenching

It's important to understand how to control the heat you're creating in the forge or oven. You'll also need to have a quenching tank where you can cool your blade in water or oil after you've shaped it to your design. The type of quenching tank you use depends a bit on what you're making. For example, traditional Japanese swords used horizontal troughs for quenching. The material needs to be made out of something that won't burn or melt if it comes in contact with hot steel. A metal barrel could work, but if you're making smaller knives, so could an old fire extinguisher body made from stainless steel.

With quenching, you're rapidly cooling the metal, and you're doing this to obtain certain desirable characteristics like hardness. When you rapidly cool steel, it undergoes certain microstructural changes that convert it into Martensite which is much harder. Most people use some kind of liquid to quench knife blades, usually oil or water, but it's also possible to use brine which is water containing dissolved rock salt.

### Water Quenching

This works well because it cools the steel faster, but there are absorbed gases in water that will bubble out when the hot metal is quenched. These bubbles can work to soften the steel and cause subsequent cracking or warping.

### Brine Quenching

Brine reduces gas absorption in the water, thereby preventing the bubbling. This results in an improved surface wetting and cooling rate, and that works to promote uniform cooling. The problem is that high carbon steels, such as those used for making knives, and low alloy steels can be uneven in their cross-section, and if you use brine to cool them, it can lead to stresses and even cracking.

Brine is also not suitable for cooling non-ferrous metals because of the potential for corrosion. For these reasons, both water and brine are typically used only for those workpieces that are relatively simple in their shape and are made of steels with low hardness.

### Caustic Soda

Using caustic soda in water provides a faster cooling rate than just using water, and this is a suitable method for some kinds of steel, but it is never used for nonferrous metals.

### Mineral Oil

Oil is another material you can use to quench your knife. It is suitable for high-speed steels as well as for oil-hardened steels. In fact, it's better overall or any steel that needs a certain degree of hardness. That's why many knifemakers prefer to use oil for quenching their blades. It has, however, a slower rate of cooling than water or brine, although it is faster than air.

If you're using oil, you'll want to make sure that water does not build up in the bottom of your quenching tank as this can affect the quenching process. Additionally, if you are working with no-ferrous metals, you'll want to use another material.

There are many oils that can be used for this purpose, but mineral oils really show the best capacity for alloyed steel. They are more costly, however, and they are not biodegradable. Additionally, oxidation of the oil can occur at high temperatures, and that can lead to the buildup of PAH—polycyclic aromatic hydrocarbons—which are toxic. That's one of the reasons you'll want to wear a respirator during the quenching process.

### Vegetable Oils

Vegetable oils are an alternative to mineral oils, and they are biodegradable, non-toxic, and relatively inexpensive. Additionally, they come from renewable resources. For those reasons, they have become more popular quenching agents. Their effect on hardness, impact strength, tensile strength, yield strength, and percentage elongation all varies, however, with the type of vegetable oil you use.

Olive and palm kernel oils reduce hardness values, but increase toughness. Peanut oil and canola oil both have high flash points which is something that is good for quenching. If you're using these oils, you'll want to preheat them to 120 - 130 degrees Fahrenheit to get the best results.

## Chapter Summary

In this chapter, we've discussed your heat sources for forging and heat-treating metal. Specifically, we've covered the following topics

- The tools you need for working with hot metal;
- The various sources of heat for metalworking;
- How to make your own heat-treating oven;
- How to make a DIY forge;
- Choosing the fuel type for heating your blade;
- Quenching materials for cooling the hot steel.
-

In the next chapter we'll discuss each step of making a knife.

# KNIFEMAKING

# CHAPTER SEVEN

# STEP-BY-STEP BLADESMITHING

Now that we've covered the basics of designing your knife, choosing your steel, preparing a heat source for treating and forging your blade, and the tools you'll need for the job, it's time to go through the process of actually making a knife. We'll take it step-by-step.

**Producing the Knife from the Blank**

First ensure that the metal piece you have to work with is large enough to make the knife you've designed. You can take some grid paper and trace the outline of the metal blank on the paper. Then, you can draw or transfer your knife design onto the grid paper. You should draw it to scale. You also want to make sure you leave enough room for the handle. You can take a ruler and grab it like you would a knife and see how much space your hand requires. For most people, your handle will require at least 4.5 inches on a full-sized knife. Most blades will be between 4 and 7 inches in length. For your first knife, it's best to keep it on the smaller side since that will reduce the amount of grinding you'll need to do.

Now that you've made sure you have enough metal for your design, you can trace it or glue it onto something sturdy enough to grab onto, such as a piece of scrap plywood. When you have it drawn or glued onto the wood, but that out. You want to make sure you get a real feel for the knife. If it feels 'off' somehow, then you might consider modifying your design. If, on the other hand, it feels right to you, then it's time to trace that final shape onto the steel blank. You can do this with a scribe, sharpie, or chalk.

Once you've transferred the design to the metal blank, now it's time to cut it out. There are several ways to do this, but the idea is to cut as much as you can at this stage so that you'll save yourself some work later on. Still, this will be a really rough draft here. Start by placing the metal blank in a vice or clamp and tightening it up. You want to put something between your vice and the metal so the vice doesn't leave impressions in the soft metal.

You can then use a grinder or power saw to cut out the knife from the blank. If you do that, you'll want to dip your blank in icy water occasionally to cool the metal so it doesn't develop a hard edge. You don't want that at this point. Also, don't hold the saw blade in one spot for long to avoid overheating that area of metal. You can also cut out the knife manually.

The best tool to use for manually cutting out the knife from the blank is a high-quality hacksaw. You'll end up making numerous cuts, but you'll get it done. Don't worry about getting the curves just right because that will be accomplished later on with files. Another way to approach this is to drill holes around the shape and then simply connect the holes with the hacksaw. In fact, you can drill these holes and then use some screws to secure the blank to your workbench while you cut. If you do that, be sure to use some oil on the metal as you drill.

**Drilling the Knife Blank**

Once you've cut out the rough shape of your knife, it's time to drill holes in the tang for the pins and lanyard hole if you will have one. Pins embedded into the handle will strengthen your knife and the connections to the scales. A common material used for these pins is brass. You want to choose two or three spots on the tang for the pins and mark them with a sharpie. Then, you can center punch them to create a small indent for your drill bit. Don't place the pins too close to where the handle meets the blade. Once you've got the indents, drill the holes with a bit that's the same size as your pin material. If you'll have a lanyard or rope, this is when you would want to drill that larger hole. You want to do all the drilling before you heat-treat and harden your knife.

Many knifemakers will also drill holes throughout the tang in order to remove some metal so that they can reduce the weight in the handle. That will also help the epoxy bond when you use it for making the handle. The holes give it a place to sit while bonding to the scales. If you do this, just be sure to leave enough metal between holes so that you don't jeopardize the strength of the knife.

**Getting the Final Knife Shape**

By now, you've got a rough cut for your knife, and it's time to start refining the shape. Start by securing the blank in your vice or on your workbench with a clamp. If you drilled tang holes, you can also screw your knife to the workbench.

You'll want to begin with the coarsest file and start scraping away the metal around the blank with the goal of reaching your original outline. You'll likely have to use a variety of files to get around the tight spots and curved areas. For those hard-to-reach areas, you can attach coarse sandpaper to a dowel. If you cut out your blank by hand, you'll probably have rough edges all around the outside of the knife. To smooth those, use a file along the outer edge, draw it flat while moving it back and forth as you go along the perimeter. You want to create straight edges as you remove the rough spots. You want the final shape to be smooth.

As you work, you'll want to periodically remove the blank from your vice or workbench and grip with your hand. This will help you get a feel for how it holds, and if it doesn't feel right, you might need to make some adjustments as you go along.

# KNIFEMAKING

## Grinding the Bevel

Your knife is now at a point where it is refined and cleaned. It's time now to grind the blade's bevel to start giving it an edge. The blade's grind refers to the profile of the blade, so if you were to point the knife directly between your eyes, what shape would you see? Another way to think about it is if you made a slice with your knife into something like clay, what shape would the cut make? Would it be a V shape or would it be like a chisel shape?

As you grind the knife down from the original rectangular shape, you're going to create bevels which will eventually meet at a point and form the cutting edge. So, depending on your knife's purpose, that cutting edge could be one of several different shapes. Let's look at the possibilities.

- **Full Flat Grind**: This is the classic V shape, and it is created by grinding the blade all the way from the cutting edge to the spine in one long bevel. This removes a lot of the metal on your blade, so it's more work, but it results in a sharp end. That's good for cutting, but it comes at a price because the more acute the bevel, the less durability the edge has. For that reason, it's common to grind a small, secondary bevel along the cutting edge, but with that, the knife will be lighter and won't hold up to heavy use for long.

- Most of your kitchen knives are likely flat ground which makes them easy and quick to sharpen, but this edge sacrifices durability and resilience.

- **Sabre Grind**: This is also called the 'zero sabre grind' or the 'Scandinavian grind.' This is a flat grind, but the bevel doesn't extend all the way to the spine. Instead, you grind about the middle point of the blade. That gives the top part of the blade uniform thickness which adds strength and weight. These kinds of blades are suitable for military and other heavy use. Like the flat grind, there is a secondary bevel on this grind, but the traditional

'Scandinavian grind' only has one flat bevel that extends to the midline whereas this sabre grind has that secondary bevel.

- **High Flat Grind**: This is a hybrid of the full flat grind and the sabre grind. The difference is that the grind goes a little higher than the center line, but it still doesn't go all the way to the spine. That allows the blade to retain some of the weight and strength that the sabre grind has, but it allows for a keener angle than what the sabre grind achieves.

- **Hollow Grind**: This has a sharp, but fragile concave bevel which is often seen on straight razors. It makes it really sharp, but also very fragile. Straight razors, for example, need constant stropping to maintain them. The inward facing bevel of the hollow grind can extend the entire length of the blade or just a portion of it. This type of grind is common for skinning and dressing knives like the Bowie knife. For beginners, this probably isn't the best grind to use because it is difficult to achieve and only has a very specialized use.

- **Convex Grind**: This is also called the 'axe grind,' or 'Hammaguir.' It is the opposite of the hollow grind in that the edges bow outward instead of inward. It kind of resembles a clamshell. This is designed to keep as much metal behind the edge as possible and still maintain an effective, honed cutting edge. That makes it a stronger edge for resisting impacts and when you're using it to chop wood, for example, it will reduce drag as it splits the wood. This is not a good grind if you're looking for something to slice rather than chop. You typically produce this grind by slackening the belt on a belt grinder. It's a difficult grind to create, and it's hard to maintain and sharpen too.

- **Chisel Grind**: This is also called a 'zero bevel grind' or a 'single bevel grind.' As you probably imagine, this is a chisel edge. It is flat on one side and on the opposite side, there is a 20 - 30 degree grind that extends approximately halfway up the blade to the spine. It makes for extremely sharp chef's knives, and you also often see it used in Japanese culinary knives. If you're going to use this grind, you want to think about which is your dominant hand since the cutting edge will be on the same side as your dominant hand. So, if you're right-handed, the cutting edge will be on the right side, and if you're left-handed, it's on the left side. In some styles, the flat side is ground in such a way as to be slightly concave so that it reduces drag and stickiness which helps food to separate more easily. This type of style is called the urasuki style. But, food is not all this kind of grind is good for; it's also very practical for working with wood. The edge is very sharp which means it will need to be maintained and sharpened more frequently than other grinds.

- **Double Bevel**: This is also called a 'compound bevel.' This is like a sabre grind, but the bevels on each side are elongated and extended further up the blade. The benefit of this style is that the blade is resilient and resists chipping and rolling. But, this increased durability comes at the price of reduced sharpness. The back bevel of this edge helps improve the knife's cutting ability since it's thinner and more acute as compared to the straighter back of the sabre grind. This type of grind is commonly used on Japanese swords like katanas. This edge reduces drag which is why a katana can slice with such ease. In Western culinary styles, the double bevel is often created with an edge bevel angle of 15 degrees while the back bevel has an angle of around 30 degrees.

As you can see, deciding on the grind means considering numerous factors including the weight, strength, sharpness, durability, drag, and intended use of your knife. For the beginner, you'll want to look at the degree of difficulty in creating the grind first, and then decide based on the knife's intended purpose. Generally speaking, the more acute the angle of the grind—that is, the closer it is to 0 degrees—the sharper the knife will be and the better it will cut. On the other hand, that means you will sacrifice weight and strength which will reduce the overall durability.

Once you've decided on the type of grind you want, it's time to create a line of reference in the middle of the blade thickness to indicate where the cutting edge will be. You can use a colored sharpie to color in the whole thickness of the blade. Then, you can take a drill bit that's the same thickness and run it along the colored edge to use the point to scribe a line. When you do that, you'll have a crisp line in the middle of the blade that you can use for a reference for where the bevel will be. It doesn't matter what kind of bevel you're using, the two sides will meet at this line to form the cutting edge. Before starting, you'll also want to coat your knife with layout fluid to be sure you've grinded and sanded all the parts of the blade later on. A layout fluid is just a quick-drying fluid used for marking patterns and color coding on sheet metal.

After you've done that, clamp the blade in your vice or attach it to your workbench with the blade out. Then, begin to file from the cutting edge toward the spine. The file will only remove metal when you're pushing on it, so when you draw back, lift it up. Keep your file at approximately a 22 degree angle as you work. The more acute the angle—like around 17 degrees—the sharper your knife will be, but remember that it will also be more delicate. This kind of angle is better for things like fillet knives and razors. The higher your angle—like say around 28 degrees, the better suited your knife will be for heavier use like cutting rope or chopping wood. You want to keep your angle between those two angles (17 and 28 degrees) for kitchen cutlery and hunting knives.

It's also a good idea to move around consistently and after several strokes, switch sides. You really want to take your time with this step. It requires more caution than it might seem at first. If you screw it up and grind too low, you'll have to restart a new edge. It can help to use a jig to control the file's movement and angle, especially for beginners. You'll continue this grinding process the whole way for both sides. Be sure to keep an eye on the middle line that you scribed in with your drill bit. This part of the process will be a lot of work, but when you get it done, you should have a clean, consistent bevel on both sides of your knife blade.

If you're experienced and can afford to do so, you might want to opt for a power tool like a belt grinder to create the bevel. If you choose to do that, you'll want a machine that is 1 X 30 (which means it has a belt that is 1" wide and 30" long) or a 2 X 72. This will be able to quickly remove the metal. For maintaining the grinding angle, many knifemakers will rig up a jig—which is just a device that holds your work in place—for use on their grinder.

If you're hand filing, a good tip is to avoid drawing your file back and forth as you grind. Your file will only be removing metal when you're pushing it away from you, so just lift it up as you draw it back. It's also at this point that you might want to create a decorative spine for your blade. There are a number of styles to consider. Try googling jimping to see one common style. Jimping is just a series of small, decorative notches that you can put in the spine.

# KNIFEMAKING

**Sanding the Blade**

After you've finished grinding the blade, you'll want to sand it to give it a bit more of an edge before you heat-treat it and the metal hardens. This is also where you'll want to sand anything that needs more of a fine finishing, like those decorative notches you might have put in the spine.

As you get started, one good tip is to duct tape the back of your sandpaper so that it won't be as likely to rip, and you can extend its life greatly. Clamp your blade down flat on the workbench, and then wrap a 60 or 80 grit sandpaper around some kind of solid structure like a wooden block or a paint stick. Without any backing, sandpaper can be very difficult to use for this purpose.

Begin sanding the bevel you just filed. Sand diagonally in one direction across the blade. Keep going until the metal is smooth, then flip the blade over and start on the other side. Once you've finished both sides with a coarse grit, go to the next highest grit, and start sanding in the opposite direction until all of the previous sand marks are gone. Keep moving up to higher grits in order to produce a finer finish and remove roughness created by lower grits. You'll want to go up to 220 or so to get the smoothest finish and ensure that any previous sanding marks are no longer visible.

Try looking at the blade from different angles to ensure you've removed all sanding marks. The light can hide those, so changing the angle helps. You'll do another sanding as well as a sharpening after the blade has been heat-treated and tempered. Do a final check of the blade to make sure that you have fixed anything you don't like and removed any rough areas. After you heat-treat the blade, it will be much harder to change anything.

# KNIFEMAKING

## Heat-Treating to the Critical Point

Just as there are different ovens, forges, and kilns, there are also different ways to heat-treat your blade. How you do it will vary based on the steel you're using and the equipment you have available to you. With that said, this guide will give you the basic information you need to heat-treat your blade. Be sure to check for any specific information you might need for the type of steel you're using. The basic procedure is as follows.

- **Heat the Forge to the Critical Point**: The critical point is different for different types of steel, but it's going to be somewhere around 1450 degrees Fahrenheit.

- **Heat the Blade**: Use your industrial-sized tongs to hold your knife and stick in the heat. Heat it until it is a cherry red color, which normally takes between ten and fifteen minutes. If you need to lengthen this process, you can pull the knife out of the heat to cool it periodically. This can make it easier for the metal to undergo the transformation that heating causes.

- **Check the Magnetism**: Keep a magnet near your forge so you can test the polarity of the knife. If it is still magnetized, you'll have to put it in longer. You want to heat the metal the point where it is no longer magnetic. That is the critical point. Some types of steels should be held in the heat for four minutes or so after they hit the critical point, but other types of steel, like the very common 1095, need to be quenched immediately when they hit the critical point. If your blade begins to glow a yellow color, it's too hot, but you should check the heat-treating requirements for your particular steel.

### Quenching in Oil

Quenching is how you will rapidly cool your knife. You'll want to prepare the container of oil prior to beginning the heat-treating process. Normally, it will take approximately two quarts of whatever kind of oil you're using. Remember that the container should be something that won't melt. When your blade reaches the critical point, you'll quench it in the oil, but don't stick the blade in all at once.

You'll want to heat the oil a bit to reduce the severe reaction and shock to the knife. Ideally, the oil should be about 150 degrees Fahrenheit before you fully submerge the knife in the oil. You can heat the oil a bit by dipping some heated scrap metal into the oil or you can dip just the tip of your knife into the oil. When the flames die out, you can lower a little more of the knife in and wait for those flames to die down. When they do, you can lower the rest into the oil. While you do this, you should have a fire extinguisher handy just in case.

Once the knife is fully submerged, you can then swish it side-to-side slowly and in a horizontal position as it cools. Leave the knife in the oil for 30 seconds to a minute, and then, you can dip it in some water to bring the temperature down to the point where you can hold it.

One alternative method for heat-treating involves 'normalizing' the blade once or twice before heating it to the critical point. Normalizing it means you are warming it up so that it won't warp or crack when you heat it to the critical point. To normalize it, heat the knife to a dull cherry color and then take it out of the heat and let it cool. You can do this once or twice and then proceed with heating it to the critical point. This is optional, but many knifemakers like to do it.

Once your knife has been heat-treated and quenched, you'll be left with something that is not very pretty and very hard. Don't worry, that's just what's left of the scale and the built up carbon, and you're going to scrape that off. If you use your file to slide against the knife at this point, you'll notice it sounds different than it did before, and you'll also see that your file bounces off the metal. This is because the metal is now much harder than it was before.

At this point, you'll want to clean the blade using soapy water and coarse steel wool or sanding paper. Be careful handling the blade at this point because it is very brittle. You should treat it like it is made of glass. Don't worry about that—that's normal, and you're doing to temper it next which will make it tougher and less fragile.

**Tempering Your Knife**

The heat-treating step you just did has made your knife very hard, but also brittle and very susceptible to cracking and/or breaking if you drop it. You'll need to soften it in order to add flexibility so it won't shatter. You want to achieve a Rockwell hardness score of between 53 and 63.

Tempering needs to be done within about an hour of the heat-treating, but you do need to let the blade cool to room temperature first. You'll want to heat the blade for tempering in accordance with the characteristics you hope to achieve. When you temper at a higher temperature—around 650 degrees Fahrenheit—you'll get a blade that's slightly softer, but tougher. If, on the other hand, you temper the blade at a lower temperature—around 375 degrees Fahrenheit—your blade will be harder and better able to maintain a sharper edge. So, for example, if you're making a chef's knife that will be used solely for slicing food, then you'll want to temper it at higher temperatures, but for heavier duty use, you'll want to go with lower temperatures.

To begin, remove any leftover carbon from the blade using 180 grit sandpaper. Wipe off any excess chemicals with acetone and a rag. If you do have more leftover residue, you will smell it as you do the next step, so you might want to temper the blade outside the house. Heat your heat-treating oven to the temperature recommended for the steel you're using. A good benchmark is around 450 degrees Fahrenheit. When it's heated up, put your knife for approximately one hour. This is where you'll smell it if you didn't get all of the oil and carbon off the blade, and it will also create a great deal of smoke. After the hour is up, take the blade out of the oven and let it cool to room temperature. Then, repeat that process again for another hour. This will yield a Rockwell Rc of approximately 59 degrees. Once this second tempering process is complete, you're ready for the final sanding.

**Final Sanding for Finish**

Once you have finished heat-treating and tempering your blade, you're ready to complete the final sanding prior to attaching the handle. You'll want to begin by grabbing a wooden block and a piece of high grit sandpaper. You'll use the same grit as that you ended with before you hardened the blade with heat-treating. This should be approximately 220 grit.

You can do either dry or wet sanding, and you'll begin with the same technique as you did before, You'll start with somewhere around 220 grit and move onto higher grits after you've sanded away the grits marks left by the previous sandpaper grit level. You should wipe down the blade between grits so that you're sure you haven't missed anything. Depending on the finish you're hoping to achieve, you'll end your sanding with somewhere between 400 and 800 grit sandpaper. With 400 - 500 grit, you'll get a satin finish, and with grit in the 800s, you'll get a polished, mirror finish. When you get to the last sanding grit, change your direction for sanding so that you're going straight along the blade lengthwise. That will give you a nice finish.

At this point, you should really pat yourself on the back. You've got a nice knife blade, and now that it's sanded and looking good, it's time to create and mount the handle. That's what we'll cover in the next chapter.

## Chapter Summary

In this chapter, we've discussed the process of making your knife blade. Specifically, we've covered the following topics:

- Transferring the design to the knife blank;
- Producing the knife from the blank;
- Drilling the knife blank;
- Producing the final knife shape;
- Grinding the bevel;
- Sanding the blade;
- Heat-treating and quenching the blade;
- Tempering the knife;
- The final sanding.

In the next chapter you will learn how to create a knife handle and sheath.

KNIFEMAKING

# CHAPTER EIGHT

# CREATING A KNIFE HANDLE AND SHEATH

Now that you've got your blade how you want it, it's time to add the handle and sheath. This is an important part of your knife that will make it much more usable. It's also an opportunity to add more decorative elements if you like. Let's start with the basics of the handle.

**Sizing the Handle**

You'll want to begin by finding some good hardwood or the synthetic material of your choice. If you use wood, it will be important to make sure the wood is completely dry. To ensure that, it should have been in a warm, dry place for 6 - 12 months. You'll want to get a piece of wood that's larger than what the final handle size will be. It should be between 1/4" and 3/8" thick. If you manage to find two pieces, you can move onto the next step. Otherwise, you'll need to cut the block in half. These are your two scales. If you're having trouble finding material for your handle, you can also find some pre-made or dimensioned scales on the web. That might save you some time.

**Cutting the Scales and Drilling the Pin Holes**

At this point, you'll want to cut the scales and drill the pin holes. Begin by placing the tang of your knife along the outer edge of one of the scales. This will help you avoid wasting wood. Clamp the tang and the scale together, and then, drill through your pin holes (in the tang) and into the scale. It will help to put scrap wood under your scale as backing so that you can reduce splinters and cracks as you drill your pin holes.

Once you've drilled the pin holes, trace the tang shape onto the scale with a sharpie. After you've accomplished that, remove the clamp and repeat this procedure with the other scale. After both scales have been drilled, cut out the rough shape of the handle in the scales with whatever tool is appropriate. You might use a hacksaw or band saw, for example.

You might also choose to drill some small recesses into the insides of the wooden scale to help create a better epoxy bond with the blade. If you do this, make sure they are shallow and don't penetrate the scale completely. Like you might have done with the tang, this will allow the epoxy to stay in the space rather than being squeezed out when the scale is clamped to the blade. That will create a stronger bond.

## Cutting and Inserting Pins

There are different materials that you can choose to use for your pins, but whatever you use should be strong and match the material you chose to use for the handle. Brass rods are a popular option, and you can find these at any hardware store. Whatever material you choose, before you insert it into the scales or tang, sand down the ends with 80 grit sandpaper to help make them smooth for a seamless entry into the wood.

# KNIFEMAKING

Once you've got the pins ready, insert them into the pin holes through the scales and knife. With a sharpie, mark the cut line approximately 1/4" higher than flush. You want to cut the pin with a little extra bit of material so that you can then file and peen it down later. After marking the pin, remove it, and cut it to size using a hacksaw. Then sand down the new end of the pin and repeat this procedure for all the other pins.

## Sand the Handle to Shape

Now that you've got the pins ready, you'll want to sand and shape the handle before attaching the scales to the blade. It will be more difficult to do that after the scales have been permanently attached to the blade. To sand the handle, leave the knife out, but put the pins through the scales of the whole handle and clamp it back into your vice. Now that the two halves are together, you can file and sand them more evenly.

Begin by roughly sanding the handle to make the two scales uniform in size and shape. Shape the front-most part of the handle where the blade and handle meet to get it like you want it. It will be very difficult to make any changes once it's attached to the knife. It doesn't need to be perfect, but get it close to what you want and you'll save yourself some time later on.

Once you've got the scales roughly sanded and shaped, you'll need to lay down a large piece of sandpaper and sand the inside of each scale. You'll want to make sure that they are very even and flat since this side will be attached directly to the tang. When you've done that, you're ready to glue the scales to the tang.

### Glue the Scales to the Tang

Depending on the pin material you chose, you might have solid metal or hollow tubing. If you have hollow tubing, you can peen the metal and embed it into the handle so that it will be better attached to the blade. In this case, pins and rivets are optional, but you will need epoxy. That will strengthen the mechanical bond and stop moisture from getting in between and causing corrosion on the tang.

To begin, tape down some parchment paper to a clean surface on your workbench. Remove the pins from the scales and separate the scales from each other. Mix up the epoxy so you can start the gluing process. Before applying anything to the tang, you'll want to degrease and clean it with soapy water and either a toothbrush or rag. If you have acetone, you'll want to use that to remove any excess oils.

Rinse the tang and wipe it dry as it's important for the epoxy to work properly that the surface be clean and dry. You will want to protect the blade area from the epoxy, and to do that, you can tape it with masking tape. Cut off any extra tape with an X-ACTO knife. The tape will not only protect the blade from the epoxy, it will help protect you from the blade.

Next, insert the pins into just the tang of the blade. Mix up your two-part epoxy on the flat surface or you can use a plastic cup. A popsicle stick is great for applying epoxy to the pins and tang so you might want to have some on hand. Apply the epoxy to the inside of the scales while the pins are still in the tang. Attach the scales to the pins with a rubber mallet so you can get them tightly into place. You'll want to leave 1/8" of the metal rod sticking out on both ends, however.

Once you have the handles on and the pins are sticking out, put everything in a clamp. You might want to use something that you can put between the clamps and your handle to protect it. Leather strips or cardboard are good options. Once you've got everything clamped together, you'll probably see a bit of epoxy coming out along the spine of the metal. This is called the squeeze-out, and it means you have a good, strong bond. Wipe that extra away with a rage or even some Q-tips with acetone. You can also clean up the epoxy that might be coming out around where the blade and the handle meet. Now, that you've got everything glued, clamped, and cleaned, you'll want to let it sit and set up overnight.

**Peen the Pins**

After letting things sit overnight, you're reading to peen your pins. At this point, your rods should be sticking out 1/8" on each side of the handle. You'll want to place the knife on a hard, solid surface and grab your ball peen hammer. Start by gently tapping the ends of the rods with the round side of the hammer. Move in a circular motion in such a way as to avoid hitting them right in the middle. You want the material to mushroom out. Do this for a few minutes on one side, and then, flip the knife over to do the other side.

When you get closer to the wood, start flipping the handle more frequently. Keep going until the pin's metal is touching the scales. Then, tap it some more so that is recessed into the wood slightly. Once you've done this with all of the pins, you're ready to begin the final shaping of the handle.

### Shape the Handle to the Tang

At this point, you've still got tape on the blade. Leave it in place and put your knife in the vice, blade-first. Start shaping the wood where it meets with the metal tang. To do this, you can use several different types of tools including sandpaper, files, the 4-in-hand, or a rasp. The goal is to get as close to the tang as possible without causing any damage. You also don't want to dull your tools.

To make the wooden handle flush with the metal and shaped all around, use a file. This will let you get in close, and then, when you've done that, you can use sandpaper wrapped around a wood block to sand the flat parts. You can also use sandpaper wrapped around a PVC pipe or dowels to sand the contoured areas.

### Finishing the Handle

Now you have the handle attached and shaped the way you want it, you can finish it with sandpaper. Begin with 80 grit sandpaper and start smoothing the handle and pins. In the same way that you sanded the blade, sand the handle by moving up in higher grits to achieve a finer and finer finish. You don't want the handle to be slippery, and so, you'll probably want to stop when you get to 400 grit sandpaper. You can go further if you want, but by that point, you should have a nicely finished handle. Take your time with this, and stop and check how the knife feels in your hand as you go along. Once everything is done and smooth, you can clean the handle off completely and then coat it with a few coats of tung oil while the blade is still wrapped up. This will bring out the richness of the colors and keep the handle protected.

You now have a nicely finished knife handle. There are many things you could do to decorate it, such as painting it or inscribing it, but this is the basic technique for crafting the handle. At this point, all you need is a sheath.

## Crafting a Sheath

Making a sheath for your knives is a hobby in and of itself apart from making the knife. It's a rewarding feeling to not only make your knife, but also craft a nice sheath for it as well. There are a couple of different materials you could use to make a sheath, but the look and feel of leather makes it a favorite among knifemakers. These instructions are based on using leather for creating your knife's sheath.

## Tools You'll Need

The style of sheath we'll discuss here is a simple pouch-style belt sheath. There are a many different types of tools made specifically for leatherworking, but a minimal list of what you'll need includes the following:

- 7/8 ounce vegetable-tanned leather;
- Artificial sinew thread;
- Needles used for stitching saddles;
- A Dremel tool, power drill, or awl;
- Contact cement;
- A utility knife and cutting board;
- One-handed leather punch;
- Compass or fork;
- Ball-peen hammer;
- A shot glass or heavy glass bottle;
- Various grits of sandpaper;
- Wood paint stirrer or belt sander;
- Plastic wrap or tape;
- Leather dye and wool daubers;
- Fiebings Tan Kote—a resin-based formula that produces an antique finish;
- Brush nylon fabric;

- Water;
- Pencil;
- Red pen;
- Graph paper;
- Manilla folders.

Once you've got everything together, proceed as follows:

**Step 1: Leather**—You want your vegetable-tanned leather to be of appropriate thickness; usually, 7/8 ounce leather is used. Check the leather for any marks or blemishes that might have been caused by the processing. You can find leather for approximately $50 to $75 from suppliers such as tandyleatherfactory.com, and you can make several sheaths from one 'single shoulder.' Just as a general tip, heavier, thicker leather is good for something like an axe cover or for heavier tools. Lighter leather is better for pouches.

**Step 2: The Pattern**—You'll need to produce a pattern for the sheath. You can use the pencil and graph paper to trace a drawing of your knife. Put the knife edge on a centerline on the graph paper, and keep it aligned with the tang. Then, roll the knife onto one side in order to trace the shape of the blade. On that tracing, draw your intended pattern leaving minimally 0.375 inches to the edge. Once you've drawn one side of the knife, fold the paper over on itself, and trace the other side by using a light or window as a bright background. If you fold the paper over, you should have enough room to be able to put the knife in and still have good retention.

Now that you have the drawing, cut it out so you can transfer it onto the leather. Do this using your red pen since that won't show once the leather is dyed. Make certain to transfer it to the finished side of the leather.

**Step 3: Cut the Leather**—Using your utility knife, cut the leather. Watch the angle of the blade, so that you're cutting straight though rather than producing angled edges. Be careful about applying pressure when you're cutting with the finish side down, since any deep cuts on the cutting board will transfer their impressions to the leather. Once you've finished cutting it out, moisten the leather with water so that it will be flexible.

**Step 4: Glue**—Glue the loop of the belt by roughing up where you will glue the leather and then applying the contact cement. This loop will end up on the inside of the sheath, and that's what will hold it in place. Give the glue time to get tacky before you adhere the sides of the leather together. Then, allow it to set for a while before moving onto the next step.

**Step 5: Stitching**—Here, you're going to stitch the loop in place. You want to set your stitching about 1/4 inches away from the edge of the leather and about 1/2 inches apart. That will help it retain its strength. It helps to create a kind of 'shield' pattern so that the top doesn't close. That will help to make it stronger. Then, you can punch holes for sewing the loop to the body of the sheath. You can use a saddle stitch where you have two stitches passing through each hole. Then, you can melt the ends and hammer the stitching down.

Next, you can use either your fork tines or your compass to mark the hole locations on the sheath body, and then, you can punch the holes starting from the top. As with the belt loop, keep the stitching 0.125 inches away from the edge. If you use a leathercrafting fork, you can emboss the leather all along the stitch line. Embossing is where you press indentations into the finished side.

**Step 6: The Welt**—The welt in leather making is a strip of leather that helps add stiffness to the sheath, which helps protect the stitching from being cut with the cutting edge of the knife. So, this goes on the side of the sheath where the cutting edge will lie. You can use the sheath to draw another outline on the leather for where the welt will be. You'll want it to be about 0.5 inches wide. The welt can extend over the edge of the sheath because you will sand the excess flush later on. For sheaths that consist of two pieces, you want the welt to be as thick as the blade or thicker, but for this kind of sheath, it can just be the same thickness as the body. Glue the welt down on the inside of the bottom piece first, and then, you can glue the top piece so you can close off the pouch. Let the glue dry.

**Step 7: Drill the Holes**—Now, you want to drill the holes that you marked on the sheath body. You can use a Dremel tool or your power drill with a small drill bit. It's a good idea to put the sheath on top of some kind of hard backing, such as a piece of wood. You'll also want to make sure your drill bit is sharp since a dull bit causes the leather to stretch and tear the opening. That will make the holes unsightly. Take care when inserting the drill bit into the holes since it can damage the outside of the finish. Drill the holes as straight as you can, so that the stitching will be straight.

**Step 8: Stitch the Body Together**—Now you're ready to stitch the body of the sheath together. You'll want to use a saddle stitch as you did with the belt loop. The way this is done is that you use two needles that enter the same hole on opposite sides of the hole. That helps make a strong hem. You can begin at the bottom of the sheath and make your way up, and then, go in the opposite direction. When you've finished, you can melt the ends of the thread and 'mushroom' over the melted end. Then you can hammer down the stitching.

**Step 9: Finishing**—At this point, you want to finish the edges by sanding them. Start by working in one direction as you go along and use a heavy grit sander so you can take off the excess bits. Once you've done that, you can use a finer sandpaper to get rid of the sanding scratches. Now you can use the shot glass—or a piece of deer antler if you have one—for burnishing the edge of the sheath. To do that, you lightly wet the edges and then you rub the shot glass over the leather until it produces a glazed look. You'll have to use some elbow grease and take your time, but you'll love the end product.

**Step 10: Welt-Molding the Sheath**—To wet-mold your sheath, you'll want to coat your knife in oil and wrap it in either plastic wrap or packaging tape. Then, put the knife into the sheath and moisten the leather using water. Using your fingers—not your fingernails, but your fingers—push the leather up against the contours of the blade and its handle. If you don't want to use your fingers, you can purchase special molding tools. You can also secure your sheath in a padded soft vice or press to mold it and give it more definition. By wet-molding, you'll give the sheath a custom-fit look. Once the leather has taken shape, remove the knife and let the sheath dry.

**Step 11: Dye Your Sheath**—Once the sheath is dry, you're now ready to dye your sheath. Using a wool dauber for this purpose, cover the entire sheath with a thin layer of dye, but don't apply too much, since it can bleed on your clothes. Apply the dye away from you in one direction, and only apply it to the outside of the sheath. There is no real reason to dye inside of the sheath. Once you've completely covered the outside of the sheath in dye, hang it by the belt loop in order to let it dry.

**Step 12: Leather Protectant**— At this point, you want to apply some kind of leather protector like Tan Kote using a wool dauber. This will prevent the dye from bleeding. Once you've applied the protectant, buff the sheath with a synthetic cloth or polyester until you get it to the sheen you desire.

Now you've got a knife and a sheath to carry it in. What's more, you've made them all yourself. Take a moment to congratulate yourself on a job well-done, and in the next chapter, we'll discuss how you can maintain what you've created.

## Chapter Summary

In this chapter, we've discussed how to make a knife handle and sheath. Specifically, we've covered the following topics:

- Creating the handle design;
- Sizing, shaping, and securing the handle to the blade;
- Tools for crafting a sheath;
- Designing and creating the sheath;
- Dying and applying protectant to the sheath.

In the next chapter you will learn all about how to maintain and sharpen your knife.

KNIFEMAKING

# CHAPTER NINE

# MAINTAINING YOUR KNIFE

Now that you've made a knife, you'll want to know all about how to maintain your creation. It's important to keep the knife sharpened, as that will prevent chipping from use. Let's start with some basic tips for proper knife care, what to do and what not to do.

**What to Do for Knife Care**

These are the maintenance points that will give your knife a long life.

**1. Hone and Sharpen Regularly**

Over time, every knife, no matter what kind, will require sharpening. There are a number of ways to sharpen a knife. You can use an electronic kit or you can use a whetstone and do it manually. To properly sharpen your knife, whether for the first time or the one hundredth time, you'll want to make sure there is no residue on the blade. You can use acetone to make sure there is nothing sticking to the blade.

You can use a package kit rather than some of the commercially available knife sharpeners because with the latter, you can't really control the sharpening, and therefore, you can't guarantee a true, keen edge. The kits that are available include different grits and guide rods for sharpening every style of bevel.

Usually, you want to use a dual grit like 1000 and 6000, for example. You'll begin the sharpening process by submerging the whetstone in water and letting it soak for at least two hours until bubbles stop surfacing. As you sharpen the knife, you'll also continue to splash water on the stone.

Use light pressure and a 15 to 20 degree angle to sweep the blade across the coarse side of the stone. Start at the base and move toward the tip. After completing approximately a dozen strokes, feel for a burr on the edge by swiping your finger across the blade—not along the blade, but across the blade. A burr is just a small build up of metal that you'll grind out. What you should feel is a bit of a catch on the opposite side of where you're sharpening. If you don't feel the burr, keep going on the same side until you do.

When you do feel the burr, flip the knife over and sharpen the other side at the same angle. After you've honed both sides, grab a piece of cardboard and use your knife to cut it. that will remove the burr, but it might take about a dozen strokes.

When you've completed this, you'll switch to a finer whetstone and do some pulling strokes. Do a few on one side and then switch to the other side about 10 to 15 times. By this point, your blade should be sharp, but to finish it off, you'll want to strop the blade and hone it to perfection.

Tape a piece of cardboard to a hard surface and apply some polishing compound. Then, make sweeping strokes—10 to 30 passes on each side—and that's it! All you have to do now is rinse your knife off and let it dry. To test its sharpness, you can slide the blade across your forearm and it should slice the hairs off. You can also hold up a piece of paper and use your knife to slice it with light pressure. It shouldn't rip, it should slice through easily.

## 2. Wash After Use

While your knife is made of stainless steel or high-carbon steel which makes it less prone to rust, you still don't want to leave it dirty for long after use. If you do, the acid, water, and other chemicals that are found in food can eventually destroy the blade by leaving dark spots and rust on it. That's why it's vital to wash your knife as soon as you can once you've finished using it.

## 3. Wash You Knife By Hand

Your knife is dishwasher safe, but it's still a good idea to wash it by hand. The reason is that your hands are more gentle than a dishwasher. You're less likely to chip the knife than if you put it in the dishwasher. Additionally, by washing it by hand, you can see if there is any kind of dirt getting stuck in the area between the blade and the handle and get it out immediately.

## 4. Dry Your Knife with a Cloth

You can leave your knife to dry on a dish rack; however, it's better to dry it with a cloth right away to minimize the chance of corrosion. That also allows you to put the knife in a safe place immediately rather than having to wait for it to dry.

## 5. Store Your Knife in a Block or on a Magnetic Strip

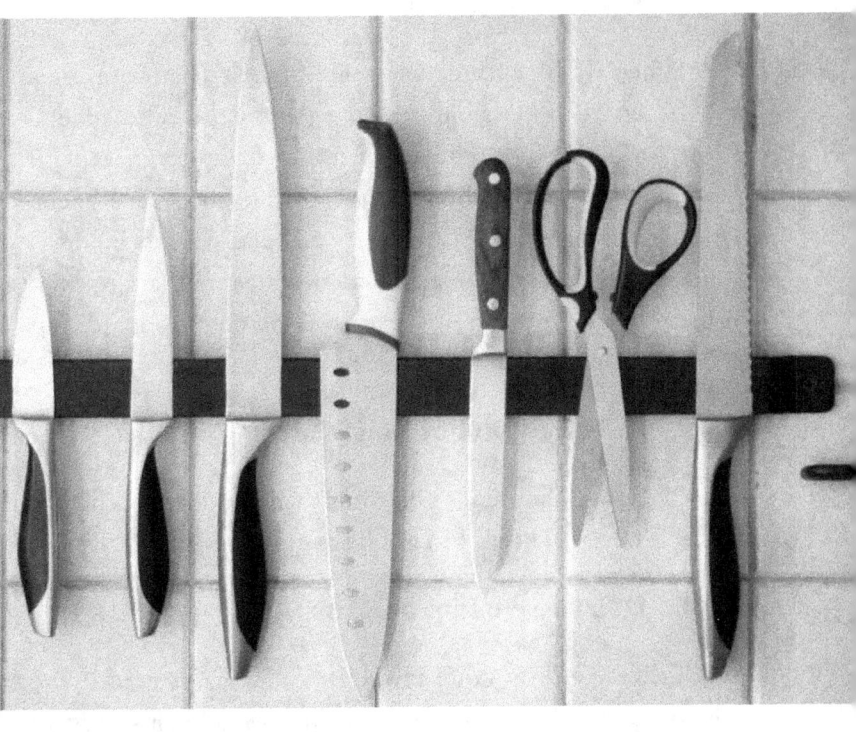

The best place to store a knife when you're not using it is in a sturdy wood or bamboo block. It protects the blade from dirt and minimizes clashing with other knives or utensils that can result in chipping or other damage. If you prefer, you can use a magnetic strip, and that will give you easy access to the particular knife you're looking for. It's a convenient way to show the blades and get to the one you want quickly. It doesn't offer much protection from dirt, but it does keep the knife from clashing with other knives.

### 6. Always Use a Cutting Board

When you're cutting with your knife, it's better to use a cutting board if possible to protect the edge. The edge is prone to damage, particularly if it comes into contact with materials it's not really designed to cut such as a metal countertop or a ceramic plate. A wooden cutting board is your knife's best friend, and it comes in sizes that are even easy to carry. You can also use a plastic cutting board, but they're more difficult to keep sanitized.

**What Not to Do For Knife Care**

These are the things you want to avoid doing with your knife in order to keep it in good shape.

### 1. Don't Leave It in the Sink

Leaving a dirty knife in the sink is a fast way to invite rust onto your knife. While the stainless steel helps prevent corrosion, when you expose your knife to certain chemicals such as those in foods such as juices or various sauces, they can cause rust. You'll typically see this starting as brown spots on the blade. Leaving the knife in the sink is a great way to make it rusty and dull quickly.

### 2. Don't Use a Dishwasher for Cleaning

While your knife can withstand being washed in a dishwasher, as mentioned above, the rigors of the rubbing and clashing that dishwashers cause can damage the knife. It can chip the blade and damage the handle. That's why hand washing is the preferred way to clean your creation.

### 3. Don't Store It in the Utensil Drawer

If you put your knife in a drawer with other utensils, you're inviting damage. It can get chipped, and simple action of pulling and pushing the drawer can cause damage. If you have to store your knife in a drawer, make sure it is covered with a sheath for protection.

### 4. Don't Cut on the Countertop

Hard surfaces like granite or metal can ruin your knife. They can make it dull very quickly, and thus, using a cutting board is a must to protect your knife and make it last longer.

These are the main requirements for taking care of your knife. You made it, and to make sure it lasts you a long time, these tips will help you protect it from damage and corrosion. The more you follow these suggestions, the longer the life your knife will be.

## Chapter Summary

In this chapter, we've discussed how to care for your knife. Specifically, we've covered the following topics:

- How to ensure proper knife care;
- How to sharpen your knife;
- How to clean your knife;
- Tips for using your knife that will prolong its life.

In the next chapter you will learn about knifemaking as a business.

# CHAPTER TEN

# KNIFEMAKING AS A BUSINESS

You might like making your own knives so much that you would like to make it your full-time business. As a full-time business, knifemaking it is your sole source of income; however, turning knifemaking into a full-time business can be difficult to do. Probably less than two percent of knifemakers worldwide do it as their only source of income. If you're certain you want to try to make it as a knifemaker, there are several tips that can help.

**Treat Knifemaking Like a Business**

So many people make the mistake of wanting to make their hobby a business, but they really don't know anything about running a business. If you want to turn knifemaking into your full-time business, then it's to your benefit to take some courses in business management. So much of what you'll have to do as a business owner involves things other than what you're making and selling. You have to know about accounting and marketing, and many other things that can make or break even the best small business.

You'll also want professional people to help you run your business. It's a good idea to have a certified public accountant on your staff as well as someone who can help you market your ideas. If you want to be a professional, you'll need to surround yourself with professional people.

**Invest in Equipment**

To truly make knifemaking your business, you'll want to have the best equipment, so you can easily make what you intend to sell. You'll want to invest in good grinders and heat-treating ovens and/or forges. You'll also want to make sure you have a proper workshop, so that you can create a sense of separation between your work life and your personal life.

**Identify Your Niche**

If you're going to make it in any business, you have to identify your niche and stick to it. In knifemaking, there are several possibilities. You can make kitchen knives or hunting knives or even heavy duty knives. Making kitchen knives is a good niche because everyone needs them and their need for sharpness means they are not as durable. It's also a heavily competitive niche. So, choose something where you feel you can really shine.

Once you have identified your niche, you'll then want to make the most of various sales events like knife shows or advertising opportunities. The idea is that you want to understand how you will introduce your knives to potential customers. This is where a marketing expert can help.

**Communicate**

As a business owner, you'll need to respond frequently and promptly to emails, phone calls, video calls, and other attempts your customers might make to contact you. You've got to be communicative, and you need to listen to your clients.

## Create Your Competitive Advantage

You have to figure out what it is that separates you from your competitors. What's your gimmick? What is it that makes you different and better? For example, you might decide to work with an artistic sheath maker to give yourself a competitive edge, or you might be the first to use a new kind of steel or handle material. Whatever it is, figure it out and then promote it like crazy!

## Delegate

It's very difficult to do everything you have to do in a business by yourself. Moreover, if you're successful, as you hope to be, then you might have such a demand for your knives that you need help making them all. That's why understanding and using the expertise of other people is a great strategy so you can do what it takes to make you happy and successful.

# KNIFEMAKING

## Professional Photography

When you go to show off your knives at a knife show, in an advertisement, or in other media, you'll want a professional photographer to capture the best qualities of your knives. It makes a huge difference in how your potential clients see your product.

## Stay Grounded

While you may be choosing to do this because it's something you love, you need to understand the basic business concepts needed to make it a successful full-time source of income. Stay enthusiastic, but also stay grounded in best practices for success.

These are some great tips to help you turn your hobby into a full-time business. Very few people are successful at making that transition, but if you're careful about doing it, you can be one of those few. You can have it all, but you have to be wise about the choices you make. The next chapter will present a few final words.

# FINAL WORDS

Well, you've done it! You've designed and created a metal tool that can be used for many different tasks. That makes you one of the relatively few craftsmen of the world today. Whether you go pro or just continue to do knifemaking as a hobby, you should be very proud of what you have accomplished.

You designed and made your own knife, and that's something that is deserving of accolades. One thing that knifemaking will teach you is that you can set your mind to doing something and accomplish that goal. What's more, as a knifemaker, you're joining the ranks of an elite group of craftspeople, and you're also now part of a historic trade.

Blacksmithing and knifemaking has been a trade for literally thousands of years, and it's one that has helped humans the world over to advance from living in caves to the world full of modern technology we have today. In fact, it's knifemaking that has probably made one of the biggest differences in the progress humans have made as the dominant species on the planet.

Very few people will know the sense of pride to be gained from designing and crafting a fine knife that can be used for many tasks. It's a great hobby, and you might even turn it into a profitable business. It's all up to you. From here, it's just a matter of honing your skills in much the same way you hone your knives. Keep it sharp!

www.ingramcontent.com/pod-product-compliance
Lightning Source LLC
Chambersburg PA
CBHW050319120526
44592CB00014B/1974